By starting your own business you will learn valuable lessons. The ideas and stories contained in this book will perhaps confirm your own ways of doing business or lure you to try and implement new ways.
Remember:
If Rozy could do it in her fifties, then you can too!

Let me help you with your business

How I made a fortune by following these three steps:

- **Motivation**
- **Marketing**
- **Management**

Ozzy

True Stories

LET ME HELP YOU WITH YOUR BUSINESS
How I made a fortune by following these three steps:
Motivation – Marketing – Management

Published by:
Brand-Wayn Publications
Fax 541 342 5278
P.O. Box 70172
Eugene, OR 97401

Printed in the USA

Copyright 2000 by Rozy Almes.
Paperback ISBN No. 96 7 9083-02
Library of Congress Catalog Card No. 00-90140

All rights reserved.

No part of this publication may be reproduced or utilized in any form or by any means, electronic or mechanical, including photocopying, recording, or by any information storage and retrieval system, without prior written permission from brand-wayn publications.

The materials contained in this book have been reviewed carefully for publication. However, the materials are intended as general advice only. Each person must depend on his/her own experience and research in using or modifying the materials contained in this publication.

The author and the publisher do not make any express or implied warranties regarding the use of these materials.

Cover Design by Vrijmoet Design

Text Design & Typeset by:
WESTERN PRINTERS, INC.
Eugene, Oregon

ACKNOWLEDGMENTS

To Jean Names whose weekly visit meant I had to write something, whose patient ear remembered all my stories and insisted on including some I had forgotten.

To my thousands of clients, many of whom I have met personally.

To the many sales representatives who worked with my company for years and became friends.

To the public in general who purchased and loved my cards and without whose acceptance and patronage the success would not have been possible.

To the State of Oregon where I had the opportunity to discover the most beautiful flowers and breathtaking landscapes. The best years of my life have been living in such beautiful surroundings.

To my friends who knew me when I started and have been true friends in good and bad times.

To the United States where you can become a success by having just one product.

To the many professional people who helped me all along with advice.

To the United States where you can call directly to the Head of Chemistry of a large corporation and ask for advice. Their willingness to help and assist is appreciated; everyone is approachable.

What an experience! Nowhere else but in the United States! Thanks, thanks, many thanks!

Rozy

DEDICATION

To my husband whose belief in me and
unconditional moral support during all the
difficult times made it all possible.
He was always behind me,
even when making mistakes, saying,
"Trust your instincts, do what you think is best."

Contents

Preface *xi*
Introduction *xix*

MOTIVATION 1

Starting Your Own Company *3*
Bit by the Bug *6*
Motivation *11*
Press On *16*
Moonlighting *19*
Quality of Product *21*
Seconds *24*
Pride in What You Do *26*
Company Growth *27*
Who Succeeds? *34*
Smaller is Better *40*
Rest on Your Laurels *42*
Money to Start *45*
A Tight Budget *47*
First You Crawl *49*
Act Like Scrooge *53*
Investors *55*
Equipment *56*
Partners *58*
Husband & Wife *60*
Ideas *61*
Professionals *63*
Consultants *64*
Innovations *66*
An Inner Talent *67*
Rozy's Rules *68*

MARKETING 69

Hands on Marketing *71*
Consumer Base *74*
Know What You Have *76*
Before You Market… *79*
Selling Well *80*
Trade Shows *84*
Advertising *87*

Building a Reputation   *90*
Image   *91*
Pricing   *95*
Listen to Your Customers   *100*
Sales Representatives   *105*
The Best Salesperson   *108*
Why Use Sales Reps?   *112*
The "Traveling Salesman"   *115*
Setting Up the Salesman   *117*
Three Keys to Success   *121*

MANAGEMENT 123

Getting Organized   *125*
Time Management Routines   *127*
Greeting and Meeting with Personnel   *128*
Open Mail   *132*
Cleaning Up   *134*
Money Matters: Basic Tips   *135*
Money Matters   *136*
Your Checking Account   *139*
Deposits   *140*
Credit Applications   *143*
Order Processing   *144*
Collections   *145*
Cash on Delivery   *150*
Profit & Loss Statements   *152*
Hiring Employees   *154*
Training Employees   *156*
The Most Important Person   *160*
Expectations of Employees   *161*
Employee Relations   *162*
More About Employees   *164*
Inventory   *167*
Managing Inventory   *168*
Manufacture Less   *171*
Inventory Control   *172*
Shipping Suggestions   *173*
A Simple Idea   *176*
Filing Systems   *177*
Computers   *182*
Rozy's Rules   *184*
Order Form   *187*

PREFACE: A LITTLE STORY

As President of Rozy Inc.—manufacturer of upper-end floral embossed cards, using reproductions of my own designs and lithographed in four-color process on special deckle-edge paper which is milled especially for us—and with a history of 17 years in the card business, I feel I need to share with you a little of my personal experience on how this successful story began.

I believe there are many people who can benefit from my many mistakes and successful results by my telling some insights and shortcuts which may help you start your own business, along with encouragement and support for your desire to own a small business.

In 1984 I attended an Art Trade Show in Chicago, trying to sell my limited edition prints. I had been selling these prints for over 15 years, but sales had stopped. The year 1984 was a year of recession. When a recession occurs, the last item people purchase is decorative art. Result of the Chicago show was zero. This experience was very traumatic. I never had a trade show where I sold nothing; on the contrary, each one had been successful.

Disappointed and having almost exhausted our cash savings, we had only $5,000 in the bank, I phoned my

A LITTLE STORY

husband from Chicago and told him we were going to go out and try to sell the cards I had in our garage.

Some years before someone had suggested I make some greeting cards with the same paper and technique used for the limited edition prints. I made nine designs but then decided against selling them. These cards used the same art paper and same embossing, but I had to sell them for less. I felt I would be competing with myself.

Months before my trip to the Chicago Art Fair, I already felt the impact of the recession by not selling my limited edition prints. I had to do something.

Before leaving for the Chicago Art Fair, I had approached two of our best stores in Eugene with a sample book of my nine cards (white/white embossing). The first store (who, by the way, used to purchase my limited edition prints) told me, "Oh, no, Rozy, no more cards! We are swamped every day with people anxious to sell us their cards." I proceeded to open my sample book, and the buyer asked me, "How much?" I replied, $35 for an assortment of 48 cards with envelopes." She then looked at them and said, "Our store can handle this," and bought. Same story with store #2.

A LITTLE STORY

Both of these stores had contacted me before I left for Chicago asking me for more cards. They had sold them all. We were in the card business! We had repeat orders—that is the clue.

> **We were in the card business! We had repeat orders—that is the clue.**

When we have problems solutions present themselves, and at that moment we may not fully realize they are the best way to do things. Later on, we realized this was the most important marketing tool there is…sell in small quantities, sell only to specific stores, and price them right.

This became our solution. By receiving repeat orders, it meant we had a product. Now all we had to do was sell it. I had manufactured a good quantity of cards on my press, and all we needed was to purchase envelopes and packing boxes and we had a product ready for market.

We had only $5,000 left in the bank plus my husband's small retirement income. We used our credit cards for gasoline and hotel accommodations. Since our means were limited, we opted to cover first our own state.

A LITTLE STORY

Fewer expenses, close to home. Necessity dictated decisions, and this was a lucky and wise one.

We loaded our station wagon with boxes containing these assortments and we were ready for business. I had no previous experience selling directly to stores. Neither did my husband. But after the first successes where I walked out with a check for $35, I eventually lost my shyness and became a salesperson.

> **Start with the oldest equipment and work up to the newest with NO debts.**

These cards were in our garage. We could proceed and convert them into money. My limited edition prints were embossed on my "Clonkers." That meant we had our equipment, we had some stock, and all we were going to do was go out and market our product. Before telling you how we started to sell, I have to tell you the story of my Clonkers.

While living in the San Francisco Bay Area, I purchased my old clonkers in order to emboss my prints. I decided to purchase the cheapest presses possible, following my father's advice: you start with the oldest equipment and work up to the newest with NO debts.

A LITTLE STORY

Clonker #1 cost me $100. The newspaper who sold it to me was so anxious to get rid of this cumbersome machine they added all types of blankets. These blankets were used in printing etchings and were very expensive. The man asked me several times whether I wanted this old machine, and when he answered my question of whether the motor worked with "Yes," I said, "I am buying it."

Clonker #2 cost me $400. I wanted to replace #1 because it did not have an automatic stop. By then many people knew of my purchasing old equipment and someone mentioned that the Palo Alto Times had one old, fully automatic press for sale. All the newspapers were changing to plastic plates, and these mammoth machines only took up space. They even shipped it to me free. What a relief to have an automatic stop and not have to manually control the machine.

Clonker #3 cost me $300. It was very old, but it was hydraulic, which meant that the press operated up and down which would assure me of accurate registration. So although it was much less of a machine in size and was older, the fact that I could register more accurately made me purchase this one. On the previous machines registration was extremely difficult; the movable tables

A LITTLE STORY

distorted the image. By being stationary the table gave me more control. I had to pay to have clonker #2 removed.

The man who sold me machine #3 assured me it was going to work, that when we reached Oregon I would have no problem finding mechanics familiar with hydraulics who could install this machine.

> **You do not flood a market. You are selective.**

So here we were. Equipment costing $350 plus electric installation, all paid for, DONE; small inventory of printed cards, DONE; repeat orders, DONE. We were in business! Our only added cost would be traveling to sell the cards. Oregon and Eugene in particular had very few outlets we could sell to and my experience taught me that YOU DO NOT FLOOD A MARKET, you are selective.

After a few months selling these cards, I decided to have them printed in color. This meant getting involved and learning about lithographic printing, the four-color process. I had been hand coloring some of my white/white cards and realized they sold better with a little color.

No money but again a solution presented itself. I

A LITTLE STORY

owned another old press—very old —that I had obtained again in California when I wanted to develop a line of greeting cards. This was an old Chandler & Price, and I manufactured these cards by embossing them on this machine. When we moved to Oregon, my monogram cards were still selling a little, so I did pack the press and moved it to Oregon.

So, here we were— two old senior people on the road for one full year.

I had designed for that press a very sophisticated line, and as one of the sales representatives told me at one trade show, "I could only sell this stationery [it was boxed stationery] to two stores in the Boston area." Selling high-priced boxed stationery is not the same as selling single cards. I learned this when one of my excellent clients told me that her customers loved the boxed cards, but when they turned them over and saw the price, they would put the boxes back and proceed to spend even more money on single cards.

My old press was given to a very dear friend, a printer, in exchange for him printing my cards. With the machine I taught him how to operate the embossing part.

A LITTLE HISTORY

So, here we were—two old senior people on the road for one full year, selling from one small town to another. We covered 17 states by car. We stayed in budget motels and every other evening one of us had a chance to choose the TV program. Every 100 miles we changed drivers. My dear husband's patience was incredible; his support made it all possible.

I forgot to add: throughout all these years I had developed excellent relationships with my suppliers and they were willing to work with me. I still do business with them today.

WE HAD TO MAKE IT. There was no other way out. We could not give up. What kept us going were the reorders we found waiting at home after our travels. Yes, we did enclose in the assortment box a reorder form with prices and address, typed at home and photocopied. The business had begun.

INTRODUCTION
Why This Book?

We daily perform actions that become automatic after years of work. These routines are acquired and become habits based on experiences learned over time. We do not know why we do them. They become second nature. We label them "common sense," the least common of all senses.

When I anxiously wanted to learn applying color to my paintings, I realized that attending art classes alone would not do it. I opted for having a very good professional artist friend allow me to watch him work on a piece he was either commissioned to paint or for immediate sale. I spent two days watching, taking notes, and being as quiet as possible. I soon noticed certain motions he did often and when asked about them, he was not even conscious of them. It is not that teachers do not want to show you. For them what they do is just "doing it." They feel they do not have to explain, it has become a habit.

This book is just about "common sense" acts we take for granted...

Therefore, this book is just about "common sense" acts we take for granted and which are not usually written

INTRODUCTION

anywhere since they are so simple and matter-of-fact.

Recently I asked a good friend of mine about some procedures I wanted to include in this book. He replied, "My father used the same systems in his business." Well, I only heard and learned about this particular "common sense" approach when I attended a trade show and met a young couple who had quite a successful jewelry business.

When asked how many people they employed in their office, they replied, "Only one and the owner's wife." I asked his wife to explain to me how she managed with only one office person. "It is all very simple," she replied. I asked her to describe what she did from the moment she put the key in the door and proceeded to take notes.

Many of her suggestions are here which I implemented immediately. To her they were "common sense" and "routines." They were the same that my other friend's father used to do. But to me they were new.

Why Now?

The experiences I learned managing several businesses during many years in different lines of work, plus my

INTRODUCTION

curiosity to find out what everyone else was doing or had proven to be successful, made me realize that 55 years of active experience qualifies me to write a book like this one.

It may be too simplistic for some experienced business people. But I certainly had to look for guidance and help until I found these simple ways to do business. Some of these practices took a long time to learn. To my knowledge, no one has explained these simple things you must do to become successful in business. They are too basic, yet they are an absolute necessity to succeed.

To my knowledge, no one has explained these simple things...

Have you noticed how once you feel so proud discovering a new way of doing something and try to explain it to a fellow business person, how they say, "We knew this for a long time. We always do it that way." Yes, but how long did it take you to find out about this?

Of course, there are many ways to do things more efficiently, and I am always on the look-out for these.

INTRODUCTION

With the advent of computers, many of the steps I learned have become much faster and more accurate, but their basic ways are still the same as when I did them manually. The principles are the same.

Computers can save you a tremendous amount of time, save on office personnel, and keep your records in better order. They are invaluable. Yet, the understanding of what and why you do something is the same.

When my curiosity is peaked by someone doing things differently, I always ask permission to pick their brains. By the way, as a woman I found it invaluable to plainly ask people for help; men are wonderful when they feel they can help a woman, especially if you do not pretend to know it all. This has worked for me in so many ways. I learned or confirmed any questions I needed answers to. I am still learning.

What Is My Purpose?

At this point in my life I am not interested in economic gain. I can share whatever secrets or procedures I have. There is no fear of competition. My purpose is the greater satisfaction of having helped whoever reads this book and finds answers to basic and "common sense" ways to avoid pitfalls in business and become

INTRODUCTION

successful. I achieved a large degree of success in my business and am comfortably situated economically.

Maybe one of my many reasons for writing this book happened when I attended a marketing seminar for "business women." My interest in being there was, as usual, to learn newer ways for marketing or management. One of the speakers was going to explain how she managed to sell over $1,000,000 in her first year of business. Obviously, I was curious.

There were several different seminars going on at the same time. I picked two. During this particular one run by two young ladies, they asked us what kind of work we did. I answered "greeting cards," and in the back another woman answered "greeting cards" also. Most of the young attendees were ladies starting or contemplating going into business on their own.

Walking out of the room, someone tapped me on the shoulder and asked me, "Rozy, don't you remember me? I attended your seminar at the museum and because of your advice my mother and I started a greeting card business and we are doing quite well. You should have been the one giving this seminar!" That made my day.

INTRODUCTION

In the many lectures I have given, many people are shocked when they hear what I have to say. I answer their questions truthfully and, as is always the case, truth is sometimes hard to accept. But others, I hope, have gained by hearing what for me was a hard experience to learn from.

The knowledge of having helped someone is my purpose. My greatest satisfaction will be in helping someone achieve success and learn to manage their business. To know I helped in a small part is payment enough.

Hopefully this book will become a manual on how to avoid losses by doing business that ends on the plus side of the column for you.

NOTES:

Motivation
(Starting Your Own Business)

STARTING YOUR OWN COMPANY

You look at people who run their own business and you feel, "That is what I want to do above all else." That is the single motivation you must have. You must be willing to:

- Work as many hours as it takes (80 hours a week?).
- Be completely immersed in your work.
- Become a bore to friends and family. (One of my daughters once told me, "Mother, all I hear from you is business." Yes, you must have a one-track mind.)
- Sacrifice income for as long as it takes. Your business expenses come first. Anything else is placed in abeyance.
- Make a plan and follow it.

Prioritize what loans—mortgage, etc.—you will tackle first once monies start coming in. Have a list and proceed with your plan. Do not take the money that is generated in large quantities during some months and blow it. Just use a certain amount that you have determined and keep the rest for the months when business is slow.

Forget about thinking as if you have a minimum wage job. If you try to think this way, you are looking only at today. You know deep inside of you that you will be rewarded many times more once you get going.

Follow the organizational suggestions in this book, and in a year or two you will start to reward yourself in more ways than one.

Be completely immersed in your work.

I was reluctant to tell my private story of how we started, but I now feel it is important in this kind of book so that whatever I express is taken at face value. *I really experienced everything I am suggesting and telling.* Hopefully this book will be an incentive for people to start working in their own business.

I feel it would be a mistake just to concentrate on the success of my business, which I am pleased to say has been tremendous. I have to explain how difficult and mind-boggling it is to start your own business. Perhaps sometimes it is just that WE HAD NOTHING ELSE TO DO, that we persisted and did not give up. WE HAD TO MAKE IT.

You must want and need to be in business. A burning desire, an obsession is what motivates you to become

STARTING YOUR OWN COMPANY

an entrepreneur—it must be the only income you can get. Therefore, you are willing to work hard to get results. You build a business for the thrill, challenge and ego satisfaction of a job well done.

Know that the final goal is achievable no matter what problems are on the way. You learn to solve them and keep going. Just focus on your ultimate goal and you will reach it with Persistence.

Business is the most exciting game in town. Being in business, you are a gambler in life and your odds of success are quite superior to anything offered in any gambling casino.

BIT BY THE BUG

Anyone who seeks to have their own business and become an entrepreneur must have an obsessive desire to achieve it, knowing that the final goal is achievable no matter what problems are on the way. You will learn to solve problems and keep going on. Just focus on your ultimate goal and you will reach it with PERSISTENCE.

I must warn you that if you caught the bug of becoming an entrepreneur and tried it once, you are hooked for life. No way can you return to being employed or having a boss. You want to be master of your life and make your own decisions. Being an entrepreneur is not some class that you take or books you read or conferences you attend. You have that bug INSIDE YOU and you will be happy only when you do it. Sometimes you may have to try again and again, one idea after another, but you will keep on trying and one day you will make it. How big—that depends on you.

Accept and evaluate your best and worst points.

Be realistic. Accept and evaluate your best and worst points. Find out where your talents are most valuable. Yet, whatever they are, one of the main things you will

BIT BY THE BUG

have to follow, regardless of any growth, is banking, MONEY MATTERS. This is the single most important aspect for failure or success in any company.

There are many entrepreneurs who have fantastic ideas and innovative ways of improving all kinds of things. These people usually end up selling the businesses they started because they do not know how to organize their affairs and give up, overworked and with no capital.

BIT BY THE BUG

a story...

A long time ago—it seems now—when my husband and I loaded our station wagon with boxes full of assorted cards and started selling them in small town America, we covered 17 states by car. Many times I felt like quitting. It was so hard. We had no money, stayed at economy hotels and ate on a limited budget. We did this for one whole year. We agreed that since we did not enjoy the same TV programs, every other day each one of us chose a program to watch.

Without knowing, we hit on the best kept marketing secret. *First, you sell in small towns.* We learned that the hard way. It was impossible to sell in larger cities. Distances were greater and business people were reluctant to see someone they did not know who was calling on them to sell.

In small towns they opened their arms to us. I usually chose the stores I felt would like our product. I walked in and asked to see the buyer. Then, when they came, I opened my book with my samples and allowed them to flip the pages. I knew I had a sale when they asked me the price. No pushy sales pitch, no extra words.

BIT BY THE BUG

My product had to sell itself. We sold to only one store in a small town. The AAA book was our bible. We knew how many inhabitants and judged accordingly how many places to sell to. If the population warranted it, we would sell to one or two more places like one florist, one museum, one gift store, and then went on to the next town.

When our CPA learned of what we were doing—a wonderful man and friend—he kept telling me that every sale I did was costing me X amount of money. He calculated this amount and felt I was doing things wrong. Yes, I was wrong if I calculated my efforts that way. I felt that if it was just one sale, of course it cost too much. But I counted on re-orders, at least three a year. Then each sale (then an assortment of 48 cards I sold for $35) represented $105. Deep down I knew that without these re-orders I had no business at all.

Re-orders are the key to success.

This is your clue. RE-ORDERS. No amount of

BIT BY THE BUG

advertising or hype will do…only if your product "checks out" (sells well). Someone told me once that I sold so much because of my charm. No way! With charm or advertising you sell only once. Repeat business is when your product is good and sells.

I am pleased to say that at this writing 80 percent of the stores I sold to at the beginning are still with us. They have become my friends. Whenever I call directly, they recognize my accent and we start chatting. Your clients are your most precious asset. You must keep them satisfied and they learn to trust you if your dealings are straightforward and dependable.

MOTIVATION

If you think money is denigrating, get out of business. You are in business to make money. There is nothing wrong with money. Call money "success." Other people give you a medal or something else. In business your medal is MONEY. If you do not like it, get out!

You always hear that it is demeaning to talk, take actions or create controls regarding money. My answer is "bunk," without knowledge of where and what is going on with your money, you can never make it in business. Earning and making profits means that you can employ more people and create income for everyone around you. You are really becoming responsible to people who either work for you or supply goods to you. You create a circle of well-being around your business.

> **You are in business to make money.**

MOTIVATION

a story...

Years ago we had a sewing group and decided that by collecting dues we could do charitable work with these monies. One of my friends mentioned that her parents who had a successful chocolate factory left her some expensive brass molds to form chocolates. She also knew a man who had worked for her parents and who needed help.

We all agreed that we had found someone we could help and do our charity deed. The best possible way was to hand this man the molds and have him manufacture the chocolates he used to make. We would supply the money for the materials needed. He would present us with the finished product which we would either buy ourselves or sell to our friends. Then we would allow him to grow and take care of the selling part once he augmented his production.

After a few months he came to us and told us that he would prefer we simply give him the money—no making of chocolates—just give him the charity money.

MOTIVATION

This experience taught me that I can help more people by employing them directly than giving them charity. I feel I help more people by creating productive jobs that require them to give something in return for the salaries received. Something for nothing never works.

Make sure what it is you aim for. You must have conviction for what you are doing. Be proud of what you do, believe in your product.

MOTIVATION

a story...

This is the most important story I can share with you. Many years ago we had some very good friends who had their own successful business. At that time I was a housewife and was trying so hard to manage our small income. I found ways to save and did everything possible to stretch my household money.

I asked my friend how with skimping and saving as much as I did, we were not ahead at all. His reply was: "STOP THINKING SAVING, START THINKING PRODUCING. Once you produce more, saving will become less important."

What a great truth! It hit me that he was right and because of that I started thinking of ways to earn money and used my mind to create instead of clipping coupons. Yet, my experience in making every penny grow served me well when I went into business. I knew how to budget and save when necessary. It taught me the value of money. But looking ahead to create and produce made it possible.

MOTIVATION

a story...

The daughter of a very successful CEO was determined to marry this young man. Her father did not agree with her choice. Yet, she married him. Just like her father told her, he was not a good provider.

She opted to help and bake cakes and sell them out of her home. After some months of doing this, her father approached her: "You seem to be serious, therefore I am now willing to help." She was appalled and asked him, "Father, are you not ashamed to have your college-educated daughter become a baker?" "No," he replied. "When you become successful, no one cares how you make money." She became very successful with her excellent products and her husband delivered the cakes.

PRESS ON

I have a PRINTED saying that I picked up 17 years ago. I have it hanging in front of my desk and it has helped me a lot. Whenever I felt discouraged, I would read it, especially as an artist knowing how many people there are with such great talents.

<u>PRESS ON</u>

Nothing in the world can take the place of Persistence.

**Talent will not:
Nothing is more common than unsuccessful men with talent.**

**Genius will not:
Unrewarded genius is almost a proverb.**

**Education alone will not:
The world is full of educated derelicts.**

PERSISTENCE AND DETERMINATION ALONE ARE OMNIPOTENT.

Once you decide that you want to be an entrepreneur and this desire becomes a COMPULSION, then you are on your way. Be aware that success is not immediate. If it were, you would not learn from mistakes that only experience can teach you. Steady, slow growth will teach you best.

PRESS ON

a story...

One of my best salespersons once told me that she baked a special cake every year, her own recipe, and delivered it to her best accounts as a Christmas gesture. They were all delighted and it helped her get appointments.

"This may not benefit me," I told her, "but it seems to me that you have a winner. Why don't you bake 2,000 cakes instead of 200? Rent the space in a bakery and sell them to some stores in your area and watch for the results."

Subsequently she told me everyone re-ordered the cakes. Bingo! This is the way a good business is started. Demand and REPEAT ORDERS. This simplified her baking at home. She then started to think about going into the business professionally. Now here came her greatest blunder.

Her husband, an engineer, had been laid off from his job, and they decided they wanted to join forces and start this business. He approached the project like a good mathematical person does, and like people working in large companies. He attended trade shows throughout the country, found out that a "shelf life"

PRESS ON

was required, sanitary conditions had to be met, etc. This took months of study.

Meanwhile, the first enthusiasm had waned. I am not arguing that all the things he found out were not true, but he concentrated on all these problems.

My advice had been, "Start doing your cakes and selling them. Once you contact your clients in your area, which is quite large, all these problems will become obvious. Then you start solving them one at a time. Many more will appear. You cannot foresee what may happen, but if your product sells, each day you will find and solve another problem. Experience will teach you what to do.

He also argued that only one product was not enough. My father would have told him, "You start with one and then another and another will develop." The result: they never started this business, and perhaps they missed making a success of that little cake…perhaps another Mrs. Field's cookie story!

MOONLIGHTING

When starting a new business, it is not good to "moonlight." To do your job and come home to work on your new endeavor will only tire you and make you give up. You must make a commitment and ask yourself:

❶ Am I willing to sacrifice one year, two years, or whatever it will take to become self-employed?

❷ Do I realize that my new endeavor will take precedence over anything else in my life?

❸ Is my family ready to agree with this and encourage me?

❹ Will we be able to live with the minimum amount possible, to sacrifice myself and my family, depriving ourselves of things we took for granted?

❺ Will I be able to pick myself up even when things look bad?

MOONLIGHTING

a story...

For three years we worked out of our garage. We wanted to make sure that the orders were still coming and we were established before moving out. By being so absorbed in our work, there was no time to complain and we knew we had to continue. Nobody would hire a woman in her early fifties, no matter how talented or experienced. And no one would hire my husband who has retired with a disability. WE HAD TO MAKE IT.

How many times I felt like calling it quits but there was no other alternative. I had applied for jobs in my profession and was not even called for an interview. There was only one way out. Self-employed, someone said, "You are the only one who can fire you." Another saying is, "You are buying yourself a job."

QUALITY OF PRODUCT

Ideas are the beginning of all achievements. They have no tangible value until they are converted into products or actions. Then they have value. New products are seen by:

- Price
- Quality
- Innovation
- Exclusivity
- Service

Be distinct. Stand out among the crowd.

Be distinct. Stand out among the crowd.

Pick your niche and learn everything there is to know about this particular part of business and STICK WITH IT. I just heard that a major, very successful clothing department chain had suffered losses when they changed their image and tried to please a different clientele. They recaptured their standing and popularity when they went back to their original image, regaining their customer base.

Copy what you see someone is doing very well: how they design their retail store, how the reception rooms looks in a service business, the packaging your competitors are using.

QUALITY OF PRODUCT

Whenever you see something that looks good to you, copy it but with a slant. Do it with a different approach or look, similar but different.

Often I am asked where I get new ideas. Very simple: I do not sit at home all of the time. Go out and make the rounds of stores and places of business, talk to their employees. By being nice and interested you will be amazed how much you learn! All this knowledge will be assimilated in your mind, and you will reach your own creations.

Whenever your products leave your premises, you must make sure that they are the best quality. I sometimes had whole printings worth thousands of dollars thrown away when I felt the color was not right. It is painful to do, but I have to live with the look of one of my products for a very long time.

QUALITY OF PRODUCT

a story...

When I started this business, I made an initial printing where I was not satisfied with the color. I had no experience yet. When these cards were selling very well and I needed to reprint them, I asked my printer to correct the color.

That involved a press-proof on the exact paper and correction on the four-color process—quite expensive. My printer said, "Why go to all this expense? They are selling well." I replied that I could not accept something I knew was not up to what I wanted, and since I felt they would sell more and remain popular for a long time, I had to do it. Those designs are still some of the most popular in my line, 17 years later.

SECONDS

Many factories have a habit of selling seconds. This creates immediate cash flow, but is detrimental to the long standing of your business. We always stress that our clients purchase smaller amounts. We can ship within a day or two, but we prefer not to have our product on the sale table.

I once read that discounting grows faster than weeds. Also, you get your customers in the habit of expecting reductions and sales. Not a good idea at all! By discounting some products you become your own competition. Your customers may decide to purchase only those items that are on sale.

**There is always going to be competition.
You cannot please everybody.**

SECONDS

a story...

One of my sales representatives told me once that when one of the manufacturers asked her to put some of their items on sale, she would not show them at all, even with being offered a larger commission. She felt since they were not selling well, why pass them on to her clients?

PRIDE IN WHAT YOU DO

Whatever you do, you must be proud to present it, be it a product or service. Truth and honesty are keys to success. Customers learn to believe in you. You must have the best product or service.

Always admit your mistakes—to your clients, your employees, and especially yourself. No one is perfect. You cannot always win. Success is: MORE WINS THAN FAILURES. You will have failures, but try to make them smaller and less costly.

Truth and honesty are keys to success.

If you are *not* committed, if you don't follow through and manufacture the best you can, you'll be out of business. When you have a business you need tunnel vision. You must be totally involved—eat, breathe with the business. You must be absorbed in the business and committed.

Love what you do. There are approximately 600,000 new businesses started each year. Very few survive after three years, and 80 percent go under in the first five years. You want to be on the winners' side.

COMPANY GROWTH

FAST GROWTH can become your downfall. More companies go under when they over-expand too soon than any other reason. I think the best way to make this point is by stories....

COMPANY GROWTH

a story...

My first trade show in New York:

Several gentlemen stopped by my booth and asked for samples. I have a habit of NO samples. My reply was that I sold them. They were furious. The following day they came back and asked me for the price of the cards and took out a few dollars to pay me. I then returned them the money and said, "I wanted to make sure you were really interested." They identified themselves as representing one of the largest publishing houses in Europe.

A few weeks later I received an order for 10,000 units of cards per chosen design. For me this was a monumental order. I replied that I could not fill this order being such a new company. They were rightfully again furious.

Yet I was right. Experience had taught me. In order to fill their order I would have to purchase larger equipment, hire more people, obtain loans, and have a larger headache. My garage was not large enough to accommodate so much product, and my slow equipment (my "Clunker No. 3") just would not do. While the

COMPANY GROWTH

larger amount involved seemed desirable, I knew it was too soon.

And what if there was only one order? What if by contracting new employees and training them, no more large orders developed? What if this was a one-time order? Where would I get the money to pay for the equipment?

I was only in my second year of business and was still learning about shipping and organization. My base was not solid enough. A few years later I could supply these amounts or more and still generate a profit, but at the beginning, I was not ready.

COMPANY GROWTH

a story...

I learned a very expensive lesson before I started my present company. I had at that time developed a beautiful line of cards, very high fashion and very exclusive. I took the product to a trade show. One of the then major department stores became excited with this product. The buyer told me he wanted to order a large amount of these cards.

Subsequently I received a signed purchase order from the company. Since the amount ordered was quite large, I ordered paper to keep on hand. Before we went into production, I received a cancellation.

I was then out a huge amount of money and had all this paper on hand. After 25 years it is still in the warehouse of a printer friend of mine!

This lesson served me so well that now I watch who and what large companies want to order. I do not manufacture exclusive lines for large chains.

I favor loyalty above anything else. By catering in the most professional and honest way to

COMPANY GROWTH

my thousands of small companies, I am not running the risk of losing a large part of my business in one swoop.

There is absolutely no way you will appeal to everybody. There are differences with <u>upscale</u> and <u>bargain</u> seekers among clients. Your product or service cannot please both of them. Identify your niche, your market!

COMPANY GROWTH

a story...

A very good friend had recently moved to his own company headquarters. He built his own office facing a spectacular view, quiet and private. His business started to falter, regardless of how many "supervisors" he hired.

He had built this business from the ground up. He finally realized that it was better having his office facing the workers and his plant, taking more hands-on supervision in order to save his company.

**Remember:
If you do not face a problem,
it will not go away!**

COMPANY GROWTH

a story...

Several years ago a group of young talented men started a greeting card company. Their line was the most beautiful in the market. All the stores flocked to buy from them. They grew extremely fast, spent money hand over fist. Of course, they could not continue. Their major clients—the big stores—were even willing to invest and finance their company in order to keep this line alive. They had to fold.

There are many more stories like these that you can check out in your own area when you talk with other business people. Stories pertaining to people you know last longer in your mind and will help you control FAST GROWTH.

WHO SUCCEEDS?

There are three main reasons why a business does succeed:

FIRST: You must have a product that sells. Someone mentioned to me once that I sold so well because of my charm. Wrong! You can sell charm only once. Repeat orders mean you have a good product and therefore you stay in business. The same applies to advertising.

You must allow a healthy margin of profit.

SECOND: You must charge enough for your product or services to generate a profit. Do not EVER charge based on large wholesale discounts. You must allow a healthy margin of profit.

THIRD: If you have met the conditions covered above and yet you are not having a profitable business, then you need to work on the third and most important reason at this time: Management, Organization.

WHO SUCCEEDS?

a story...

At one of my lectures someone asked me what to do. His product cost him so much, and yet he had to sell it for almost cost in order to be competitive. My response was to look for another product. You cannot stay in business when you merely exchange one dollar for another. Something must be left over as profit.

WHO SUCCEEDS?

For most of the readers of this book, many of my suggestions will seem simplistic, matter of fact. I know that. It is just common sense which took me many years to learn by experience. I made all the mistakes in the book, but I learned from them.

Many successful business people do not know why they become successful. They do not stop to think or write in detail *why*. For them the processes to achieve success have become second nature and they think it is only common sense known by everyone.

WHO SUCCEEDS?

a story...

When I was learning to paint, I asked a good artist friend of mine to allow me to watch while he worked on a picture to sell. I promised to be very quiet. He graciously allowed me to do so. I was taking notes all the time. After he finished, I questioned him about certain things he did. He looked puzzled, he did not realize he was doing them. They had become second nature to him. His years of work had shown him these shortcuts.

WHO SUCCEEDS?

In this book we are talking about how to start a business, how to market, and especially Organization. Who becomes successful? What do you do after you start your business, you are marketing correctly and everything is falling into place, yet you are not reaping benefits? Your profit and loss statement is not in the plus column, or if it is, it is not as much as you expected it to be? Why? Well, my answer is Organization.

> **The more you talk with other business people, the more you learn.**

There are hundreds of wonderful success stories by people who made it, even became millionaires in their own business. What these success stories tell us time and time again is that they have reached this pinnacle because they took Organization seriously, especially Money Matters.

The more you talk with other business people, the more you learn. I am sure I still have a lot to learn. The systems we implemented in our business made us extremely effective, employing fewer people and making everyone responsible for their work.

The reason for starting a business and growing slowly

WHO SUCCEEDS?

but firmly is meant to make sure you are reaping the profits. By being completely involved with every facet of your business, you gain the experience of every part of the work needed. As you grow, you delegate more and more jobs to other people, but you know what needs to be done and how.

Ask people who had a business and are no longer working, "How did you fail?" Find out. Good and bad experiences by others are lessons well worth learning.

SMALLER IS BETTER

Too many layers of command impede work, slow down everything and when a great idea is rehashed so much, it loses momentum and importance.

The following is a very old story, but how true! (There is nothing better than a story to make a point. You will always remember the story more than the suggestion.)

WHO SUCCEEDS?

a story...

A king convened all his ministers to discuss a very important matter. Before starting proceedings, he emphasized that this job was so important that it had to be resolved fast.

He then asked his servant to bring in a large chunk of ice. He took this ice and handed it over to the minister at his right and asked him to pass it on to the minister sitting at his right, and so on until the ice chunk ended back with him.

By the time the ice reached him, it had melted almost completely. "That is what happens when too many people are involved in decisions."

REST ON YOUR LAURELS

Things are going rather well. Your sales have increased. Your personnel is reliable, and you have an easier time. Beware you do not become complacent. The world is constantly changing and there are always out there young new bright people who may come out with a better or cheaper product.

Beware you do not become complacent.

Go out and visit stores that purchase from you and ask questions and find out what is new. Attend trade shows and look for new ideas and products. Just be aware of what is out there. Sitting in your office will not give you a real overview of what is happening.

REST ON YOUR LAURELS

a story...

For many years we had very good sales representatives in a particular area. This couple visited clients and sold extremely well. Their company was very successful. The husband had joined his wife in "repping" when he realized she was earning more than he did in his profession.

Then he fell in love with his computer, hired sub-reps and stayed home managing them through telephone calls and data print-outs. They rarely visited their clients or contacted them by telephone, relying on their sub-reps. Training these new sub-reps was time-consuming, and their longevity on the job was very iffy.

Pretty soon the wonderful business they had developed just fizzled out. They began losing companies to represent. Their sales had suffered, and these companies were no longer satisfied with their performance. Their personal contact with clients and follow-up had deteriorated. They lost their business and had to start all over again.

REST ON YOUR LAURELS

Yet, we had extremely good experience with sales representatives who worked as couples. They relied only on themselves and were always treating their job as their own business. We also found out that when they had just a few good sub-reps it worked best. A very large sales organization did not prove to be very successful for us.

MONEY TO START

You do not need big capital to begin a business; the more you have, the more you'll throw out. A tight budget keeps you focused and controlled. So many new businesses are launched with great ideas. Very often these businesses fail because they bite off more than they can chew. Either they become very large too soon or try to do so much that they overextend themselves with employees, purchases, etc. and are strapped for money.

A tight budget keeps you focused and controlled.

Do not spend a fortune on letterhead, brochures, etc. when you are starting. Do not consult a public relations firm or advertising agency. WAIT. Grow your business first. When you start a manufacturing business, start with used equipment. Only buy state-of-the-art equipment once you have a solid track record and have developed a pattern of continuity. It takes time.

Yes, it is exciting to find out that your idea is well received and you can see what a success it is going to be. Then you try to make it while it is hot. I can understand that. Sometimes you just have a certain time-

MONEY TO START

span where your product is at its peak of acceptance and you want to take advantage of this.

Very often the best ideas are valid for a few years and then they become old. Consumer purchasing habits change and you want to get in at the best time, when your ideas have a new slant or you have a better product.

A TIGHT BUDGET

Be prepared when lean years happen. Nothing continues the same, either all up or all down. There is a beginning and an end to everything.

The 1980s recession was a scary experience for me. I was selling limited edition prints. At that time I realized that I had to think differently, find a new product. That was when we started selling our cards. To start a business, you do not need big amounts of money; you very often need just a few samples. Use your credit cards and finance yourself with the suppliers.

> **Be prepared when lean years happen.**

You have to discipline yourself to use just a certain amount of money. Do not go out and spend on extras while depleting the capital you need to operate. Try to always pay for your equipment in cash.

Hold off buying new equipment until you can afford to pay for it completely or at least within one year or less. You do not want to be strapped with high monthly payments having invested in a very expensive piece of equipment that you must keep working 12 hours a day or more to pay for itself.

A TIGHT BUDGET

What a relief when your expenses are only the normal ones and there are no big loans pending, nor monthly payments for that particular piece of equipment that is going to do wonders for your company. Before you commit yourself to that purchase, make sure you can pay for it outright, then you will enjoy all the innovations the machine has. Otherwise, work with your old clunkers until you can comfortably upgrade them.

FIRST YOU CRAWL...

You must become a good administrator; that is Rule #1. Even professional people have had to assign very valuable time to managing their money matters. They realize it is vital to their continuous well being that keeps them in business or their profession.

Most of what I describe in this book is meant for new businesses, the kind that start in this way:

First you crawl, work off your kitchen table.

Second you sit down, work out of your garage.

Third you walk, rent a place for your business.

Watch out that once you WALK and move to a larger space how things are placed. If you don't, no matter how much larger the space is, it is never enough. Do not spread out too much. Be niggardly about saving limited space. When you think you are absolutely choked for lack of space, then you either rent or build a larger unit.

One of the blessings of a tight budget is that every expense is thought about, reviewed many times, and decided upon when absolutely necessary.

FIRST YOU CRAWL

a story...

A friend of mine started a card company. Her husband, a successful professional, helped her with a sizable amount of capital. She told me she just kissed this capital away in no time. She advertised, bought supplies, hired more people than necessary, etc. Had she started with limited capital she would have been more careful.

First, you crawl.

FIRST YOU CRAWL

In the CRAWLING stage you wear all the hats and slowly you add personnel—only when absolutely necessary. You keep working in the garage until you see your way clear and have developed a following or repeat orders that are consistent.

At the beginning stage you do not want extra expenses, and besides, you need less space then. Repeat business is the clue to success. Without this it is a one-shot deal. Some of these one-shot deals can be extremely successful, but you want a business that will last.

> **At the beginning stage you do not want extra expenses.**

Having worked until this stage of growth in your own home and avoided expenses helped capitalize your new business. Remember, you only had one expense that covered home and place of business expenses. The money you saved is your seed money for avoiding having to obtain loans. Feeling confident of re-orders and with your business established, it is then time to move and rent a larger place of business. We worked in our home for three years before renting.

Walking does not mean splurging; far from it. Having been under such economic restraints for such a long

FIRST YOU CRAWL

time, you want to make sure that this decision, renting a space, means that you have gotten enough repeat orders to feel comfortable about the continuation of your company. Do not forget that you will duplicate your expenses, so make sure this move is based on hard numbers. Hopefully you will not need loans if you follow these organizational suggestions.

ACT LIKE SCROOGE

Try to be Mr. Scrooge during these first years: no new cars, clothes, entertainment, whatever you and your family can do without. This will free your capital to reinvest in your company and the savings of not having to pay interest on loans will be rewarded many times over.

Better put all your money and effort in your product.

You must have conviction about what you are doing. Egos are left behind when all you want is to have a successful business. The finely decorated main office, the lovely furniture, the very attractive receptionist...none of these improve your business.

Better put all your money and effort in your product! Your buyers do not care where you do your business. They care if the product arrives the way you presented it, or better. Always better.

All these amenities are very nice to have, but priorities come into play and first things must come first. Once you do millions of dollars worth of business, you can play with some extra cash. At this point, in the beginning stage, every penny is used to:

ACT LIKE SCROOGE

- Develop the best product or service you can.
- Repay all your debts.
- Take your discounts, become a discounter (that is, pay within terms on your purchases where your supplier usually gives you an additional discount when paying ahead of due date).
- Invest only after you DO NOT OWE ANYTHING BUT THE CURRENT BILLS.

The truth is that a good substantial business does not exist because of lavish offices or impressive furnishings or best location. They are known for how well they manage their business and their reliability. Have this thought in mind whenever you plan to go out and spend on image only.

In the beginning, operate in the most modest circumstances. Your salary is minimum. You start by selling your product and watch your everyday expenses like a hawk. Every penny and dollar you save you reinvest to avoid loans, and this money compounds itself many times over.

INVESTORS

Your frugality pays immense dividends. Just be patient. You can do it without outside investments which will dilute your ownership in your company and create all kinds of interference in management decisions. Just pull in your belt and spend the least amount possible. It will pay off in the long run.

Investors in your company can become quite a nuisance. How much money they invest will determine what voice they will have in running your business. You want to be your own BOSS; that was the reason you started a business. You do not want someone looking over your shoulder and criticizing. You want to do this yourself—you are your best critic.

EQUIPMENT

Try to work with equipment that may not be so up-to-date but still does its job well. Be careful not to accept the advice of equipment sales agents who show you how you can save time and employees by purchasing their latest gizmo. This gizmo or new piece of equipment has a large price tag attached, but you can purchase it by renting and paying for it in installments.

DO NOT FALL FOR THIS! I bought my paper cutter only when I realized I could repay the cost of the new machine within one year, by saving on what it cost me to have the paper cut by another company. Only then did I invest in this expensive piece of equipment, and I paid cash for it. NO LEASES OR MONTHLY PAYMENTS.

EQUIPMENT

a story...

A good friend of mine who had a typesetting business, a very gifted and wonderful person, asked me, "Rozy, how come I work so hard and yet make no money?" My answer: "There are two reasons you are not generating money. First, you may be charging too little for your services. Second, your organization (monies, employees, supplies, especially equipment) are not under control.

She was constantly upgrading her equipment with loans, and every time she was obligated to spend money on newer machines. Yes, they were faster and more accurate, but the monies she had to spend were more than what she was being paid.

My suggestion was to reduce her expenses, move her business back to her home where she did generate income when she started, start all over without the latest equipment, work longer hours with no big loan payments over her head, until she had the cash to pay for the new wonderful equipment.

PARTNERS

Some people like company and start a business with a partner, usually a friend, since the initial part of planning is so exciting! I prefer no partners. Any mistakes made are my responsibility, and any brilliant or foolish ideas are mine alone. I do not like to feel that someone else is responsible if things go bad.

Avoid partners like the plague. You will have enough problems without adding the greatest one of all, a partner: another person's thoughts, decisions, and looking over your shoulder wondering whether you put in as many hours as they do, etc., etc., etc.

Avoid partners like the plague.

Of course I know how big a problem it is to make all decisions by yourself with no one to share your responsibilities, no sounding board. My suggestion is to walk away your problems. Walking without music, just plain walking, will clear your mind and you will be able to think positively and solve whatever your main problem or preoccupation is. You may need several walks, but it sure helps.

PARTNERS

An entrepreneur is like a puppeteer. He holds all the strings. He has the knowledge of everything that will take place. Starting and working in your own business will also help you to get out of your own self-commiseration and look forward to every waking hour of the future. Having goals in mind usually helps you find a way to overcome problems.

HUSBAND & WIFE

Husband and wife in a business: this is a very delicate subject. You had the advice of your husband/wife when you started, but working with them may create problems. Your partner has been extremely supportive and even active in your business. What to do?

Try to find an area where your partner can excel and leave it up to them completely. Define roles and responsibilities. That is sometimes difficult. Frictions can arise, and it will take a lot of thought and work to figure out solutions.

Never hire friends or relatives.

You need them because they are your most trusted support, but it is your business and you have to make decisions with a cool head.

My motto is, "NEVER HIRE FRIENDS OR RELATIVES." I want to be free to reward and dismiss. This is so difficult if feelings enter into the equation. Don't confuse employees; don't give contradictory messages. You can have only one "BOSS."

IDEAS

Knowledge in specialized topics is less expensive to hire than to try to learn all the nuances of new processes. Your time is more valuable in being creative, coming up with new ideas, controlling the business, personal contacts and research. You know that ideas are what count in business. You cannot clutter your mind with becoming an expert at everything.

You cannot clutter your mind with becoming an expert at everything.

As your business progresses, you will have specialized people do the work you did when you were counting pennies. To become an expert at something, you must perform that task daily; your worth for your company is coming up with new ideas.

Ideas are what drive a business. Innovative ideas are what makes one business more successful than another. Recently you may have read of large companies complaining that new graduates of business colleges think and act alike, all the same notions and ideas. What are always in great demand are innovation, ideas and creativity.

These observations may seem to contradict my advice

IDEAS

that you must know everything involved with your business. This is still the case, but you will let go of many of the things you did at first, sometimes poorly, once you have the means of hiring experienced, specialized persons.

PROFESSIONALS

There are two professionals who are essential to a business. Attorneys and accountants. You ask them what impact any action will have as to the laws, taxes, etc., but you decide on the business decisions. Follow your inner thoughts and desires.

Accountants should not run a business. They are number-driven, which is wonderful, but there is so much that cannot be put into set numbers, so many times when you have to take RISKS when you have that gut feeling that it must be done. When it fails or does not become profitable, then it means this was not a good way to go. You learned an expensive lesson—one that will serve you for years and years to come.

CONSULTANTS

Consultants, if you must have one, are best chosen from a small company run by a one-man show. A large company will add on hours of work with many more people involved and more questions asked and then transmitted to the rest of the group.

The best consultants are your own people and yourself. It takes time to learn your business, and coming from outside is not a guarantee they really know what is going on. As a manager and CEO of your company, make it a point to answer your telephone directly at least one day a month. You will learn more than any consultant will ever tell you. How about that?

> **The best consultants are your own people and yourself.**

Too many different departments in a company are confusing, expensive and keep ideas from moving freely and fast. These ideas are created by lazy executives who want someone else blamed if anything goes wrong. They love committees. Then if something proposed at their meeting never materializes or is a flop, they can always claim it was their committee.

INNOVATIONS

The marketplace is volatile, it is always changing. Nothing lasts forever. We are in constant flux. Perhaps when you start your business, whatever your field, at that particular time there is demand for your product or service, but do not fall asleep on your laurels. You must be alert and find out where the market seems to be going and anticipate changes. This is essential.

You must be alert and find out where the market seems to be going.

The wealth of a nation is based on innovations and creativity. This can best be achieved with small businesses. Nowadays the trend is to make progress in only the computer sciences. That is where the greatest profits and advancements are rewarded. Yet, we still need the bricks and mortar, the food, health care and all the niceties we have grown accustomed to. There is still a demand for carpenters, gardeners, electricians, etc.

No society can survive with only computers. At least not until we have devised robots to take care of all activities that we humans do so well. They have not reached the point where robots can think by themselves and lead—they are still following instructions.

INNOVATIONS

The innovation in human society is reached by single minds who do the extraordinary or find ways to do things better. When you are an entrepreneur, the first rule of thumb is either to bring out something new or improve substantially on what exists.

New ways in marketing, presentation, image, whatever makes a small business stand out. Do not forget that only small businesses can try out new products or systems fast and inexpensively.

For instance, when a small business wants to introduce a new product, the entrepreneur must go out and offer it to his customers directly. His market research is done right away: no experts, just visit your clients individually and see whether they purchase your product or engage your service. You can change prices without hurting your base. It can be done quickly.

AN INNER TALENT

Being self-employed can be painful when things do not turn out well, but when success comes, and it usually comes in small doses, it incrementally adds up to true success. There is nothing more satisfying than watching your idea reap benefits money-wise and, more importantly, build inner confidence. All the bumps you found along the way were rewarded by being independent and being your own boss, relying only on your own decisions.

It bears repetition. You must have what it takes to become self-employed. This is like talent. It is within you and it cannot be taught or acquired. It is your inner self.

One day my son came home from school and told me that he was criticized because he bossed all the other children. I told him that this was not a defect, it was an asset, but that it was one where he could not afford to let the others down. He had to be the best-informed and know more than the other children. Quite a tough assignment! Same with entrepreneurs: not all of us are born with that desire. We just must do things better.

Rozy's Rules

•

A business grows with the strictest integrity.

•

Hands-on experience is a must to be successful.
As a small business you have this advantage.
Use it.

•

Listen to your customers, build relationships.
Treat them as if they are the most important people
in the world because they are to your business.

Marketing

HANDS-ON MARKETING

Marketing at first must be done by you, the head of the company. You are the one who goes out to the marketplace to find out what is going on in businesses related to your own. You are the one who reads newspapers and listens to what is vital and new regarding your product.

You cannot achieve this knowledge by hiring other people. You would then learn only second-hand. As we all know, sometimes it is more of what we grasp by looking, hearing or just plain noticing, like when we question employees and observe how they answer. There is a certain feeling that we learn to interpret.

Hands-on experience is a must to be successful.

When you enter a place of business, subconsciously you know whether they are going to close. Perhaps it's the lack of merchandise...the fluorescent light that has not been replaced...or some other tell-tale sign that is the indicator. It is something that no one else can tell you. You *feel* it and every time that you look around, you will learn more.

Hands-on experience is a must to be successful. Nothing supplants this. Book learning is good, but I prefer to read a book on the subject after I run into a problem, hoping to find the answer and solve the difficulty. Then I look for a solution in books.

HANDS-ON MARKETING

a story...

During the year we were selling in 17 states, we saw a trend developing. In our business we saw small independent stores using different display fixtures, different layouts, and we noticed how these stores were full of people. Next to them the stores that had old display fixtures and the same old set-ups were empty.

Wouldn't it have been beneficial if the top marketing people in the large corporations had come out to the real world and seen what was going on? That is your advantage as a small business owner!

Keeping open to new ways of marketing pays off. One of our distributors from Sweden came to visit us once and told us they sold cards only in half-dozen amounts. Later on I learned that in New Zealand they sell them in ones. So we experimented and now offer choices—either dozen or half-dozen amounts.

CONSUMER BASE

We are blessed in the United States. We have a huge marketplace. There are millions of people whom we can reach without barriers, with a single language and freedom of transportation. Did you know that with one good product you can become successful here? In other countries you must have a large variety of products because there are not so many consumers. Besides, here in the U.S. we have consumers who can afford many different price levels.

The larger your consumer base, the larger your profit margin will be.

The larger your audience, the bigger your success. If you produce or offer an item or service that has a wider demand, the larger your business will become. If your product is limited to just a small market, unless its price is high enough your growth potential is smaller.

For instance, have you ever asked why sports figures, TV and movie stars, etc. earn so much money? They deserve it. They please a larger audience than a professional person or a manufacturer of certain products.

CONSUMER BASE

It is a numbers game. Everything that reaches a large audience can command a bigger share of the market. So, the larger your consumer base, the larger your profit margin can be.

KNOW WHAT YOU HAVE

Evaluate your product line all of the time. Get rid of non-productive items, no matter how much you like them. Do not allow these products to continue to take up inventory, time and attention. Just clean them up and do it fast! Instead, bring out something different. Give the new items a try and if it works, fine. If not, discontinue it. Listen to your customers who are buying your products.

> **Listen to your customers who are buying your products.**

Once you find a product that is your trademark and is the mainstay of your business, keep working it until you see this item get weaker in sales and its demand dwindles. Do not forget that everything in life is in perpetual motion and new things, thoughts, procedures happen to all of us.

Do not flood the market with your product if you want to stay in business for a long time. You do not want to sell only once; you want to have re-orders. As explained before, you have a viable product only when you receive re-orders. To make sure of that, you have to choose your customers and give them a sense that

KNOW WHAT YOU HAVE

they have something unique which other stores do not have. Put yourself in their shoes. If you had a retail store, would you rather buy the unusual and different product that's a good seller, or carry the same thing other stores carry?

The same is true for a service company. You must be different, have a distinct slant.

KNOW WHAT YOU HAVE

a story...

A buyer for a very large department store told me she never buys what sold well the previous year; she wants something *new*. You want to have a classic product that will continue selling year after year.

When you obtain one-of-a-kind of anything, your attitude towards this item is different than when you see hundreds of the same thing all over. You want to be one-of-a-kind, and do your marketing in a way that not every corner store has your product. Or your service is the same and available from many competitors.

BEFORE YOU MARKET...

The more exposure of your product, the greater success you can achieve. Let me make it clear that you must be ready to forego 50% of the retail price of your product to the retailer and 5-20% of the price to your sales representatives in commissions.

This is a must and in your mind you have to rationalize and accept why this will be beneficial to you. It is the only way to grow. Each sales person and each new client will mean more sales with less effort on your part.

SELLING WELL

Nothing is sold until it is sold well. Three principal marketing strategies in a new business with a product should be:

1) Personal calls
2) Trade shows
3) Telephone calls

My suggestion is to make personal calls, supplemented by trade shows. When your approach is personal, introduce yourself and then ask to speak to the purchasing person. Cold-calling is a difficult job. But once you do it several times, you become confident and learn how effective it can be. You must be polite and instill trust by presenting yourself in the best possible way. Clothes and demeanor do that.

The first time I approached someone on a cold call, it was so difficult and I had a tough time trying to calm myself. The second time it became much easier and so on. Now it is even a pleasure to do it!

Any size order is a beginning and can develop into larger purchases over time. At trade shows you never know who the people entering your booth are, what kind of store they have, the location, how long they have been established, the size of the operation, good-

SELLING WELL

will, etc. This is different when you cold call and choose the stores you want to approach. You then judge by their physical appearance. In time you learn to evaluate how well they are doing by their appearance and inventory. You get the "feel" of the organization.

Our policy has been to sell to just a few businesses in any given city. If it is a small town, we might try one florist, one bookstore, one boutique. No one asked us to do this, but we felt that the uniqueness of our product required avoiding overexposure. This way we remained in business for over 17 years with the same high quality product.

Any size order is a beginning and can develop into larger purchases over time.

We have a unique approach. We do not advertise. Our salespeople know that we watch very carefully where they sell because they know they had better get the best store in the area. They want to get re-orders and we will not ship if the stores are close to each other.

When a new order or request arrives, we call one of our established good clients on the phone and ask them about this new account in their area who wants to buy

SELLING WELL

our product. We want to know if this would be a problem to them.

They are very open about it, telling us if this is a store just around the corner. It may have a different street name, same zip code, we want to know. Very often it is someone opening a new store who has been checking out what merchandise others carry and managed to locate us. We then tell our clients that we just wanted to make sure it would not interfere with their business. We then do not ship. These customers have remained with us all these years.

> **Find a niche and stick to fewer stores but excellent ones...**

We sell all over the United States and export internationally. Some distributors have purchased from us over the years. Our way of doing business is not to flood the market, find a niche and stick to fewer stores but excellent ones who have been with us for a long time.

SELLING WELL

a story...

I once received an order for thousands of dollars sent by one of our sales representatives. The company was located in California, and we had not heard about them. I called one of our clients in a small town where this company had a branch and asked him who this company was.

His reply was, "Rozy, if you sell to them we won't buy from you anymore." It was a discounter organization.

There is nothing wrong with selling to these stores—if that is your niche—but in my case the thousands of dollars for this order would have damaged my consistent sales to the rest of my clients.

The sales representative who sent me the order was furious. I told her that if my purpose for being in business was to just stay for a year or two, then I would ship indiscriminately, but my aim was to last much longer, and that was my choice.

Be loyal to your customers. Know what your image is.

TRADE SHOWS

Trade shows are an excellent way to introduce a product. Before you sign on, it is best to attend a trade show. You then get the feel of it first. Trade shows can be bewildering if you go for the first time. There is so much to see that you may feel your little gizmo is inadequate and wonder whether it will sell. Do not get discouraged. After a few visits, you gain experience and zero in on items and places you care to visit again, learning about your competition.

There are so many people coming to these shows, you may wonder why they do not stop at your booth. Understand that everyone has a different "niche," different products they are looking for. When your prospective buyers show up, believe me, they know what they want.

Experienced buyers know what they are looking for. They always search for the new, unusual and different. If your product is novel and priced right, do not get discouraged if their initial orders are small. They want to test the products and make sure their decision is right.

You may have to attend the same show several times. This will show buyers who were hesitant to buy from

TRADE SHOWS

you the first time that you are still in business, becoming successful, so they are willing to give your product a try.

I found there is no need to get elaborate with decorating, displays, etc. especially if you are a newcomer at a trade show. This is extremely costly and just keeping your booth clean and showing off your product well is good enough. Later on you may invest in displays. After visiting several trade shows and learning by watching what others seem to do effectively, you can copy and modify some of their ideas with little expense.

The key is just showing your product.

At trade shows you cannot and should never judge by appearances. That little lady in tennis shoes may become one of your best customers. My approach has always been to treat everyone as though they are the most important person, which they are, and one extra smile and a polite attitude do not hurt.

Experience also taught me that investing in a booth just for your product is the best strategy. When you show together with other people's products, your items get lost among so many others. By having *only* your

TRADE SHOWS

product, you will better evaluate whether you have the buyers' acceptance.

There are trade shows in major cities close to where you live. Start with one of these. You will save on airfare and hotel since you can go home at night.

The key is *just showing your product*, plus manning the booth. By manning the booth yourself, you learn a lot from whoever stops by from the questions they ask.

If you start with too large a variety of products, you will soon find out which ones outsell the others. Then you can concentrate on the winners.

Also you hear and learn from your fellow exhibitors. But be careful: there is too much bragging and you will soon learn to seek the true lessons.

ADVERTISING

Advertising has its place, but not for a beginner. It may also distort information. You want your product to succeed in the long run. A clever advertising campaign may create a spurt of sales, but will the sales stick? Will the public continue to patronize you? Or was it a one-time-only sale? Better to go slowly and feel your way. Once you can afford to advertise, go for it with the best professionals in the field.

Our advertising budget focused on direct mailings, better displays at the trade shows, and enclosures with our product. Word of mouth and excellent sales representatives created our growth. No direct ads.

ADVERTISING

a story...

Stores, understandably, do not want to carry products that have the address of the manufacturer on their product. We have only the name of our company printed on the back with the city and state. Since we did not advertise, other new merchants went to all kinds of trouble to find us. Just a few experiences...

One day we were contacted by our Chamber of Commerce. They were very excited about an inquiry they received from a business in New Zealand who asked about us. This company is still one of our distributors. Another time, the owner of a store called the telephone directory assistance asking about us. The first operator could not give them the information. The owner was determined and called again. This time she explained the cards she was looking for. This new operator told her, "I buy them all the time," and gave her the number of one of our clients. She was so excited to finally locate us. Another customer in Eugene who was trying to find us for three years found out in Seattle that we were in Eugene. The post office delivered mail to us repeatedly with the address, Rozy's Cards, Eugene, Oregon.

ADVERTISING

Be careful when you advertise. You may get an immediate response, but after the ad stops, your sales slow down. Professional advertising companies suggest then to try to use other media, perhaps radio on a consistent basis. Remember, REPETITION is the name of the game in advertising.

You are better off with a smaller, consistent ad in your local newspaper or periodical with a clear, recognizable logo than with a larger ad running only once.

Repetition is the name of the game in advertising.

Also be specific: not "We are the best," or "We sell for less." Instead, "Today, we feature our tableware at 10% off," or "We became the sole distributors for," "Today we offer our homemade candies," "All our dolls are 10% off," "You are invited to attend classes from 'Z' about gardening." You get the message. These ads, if continuously appearing in the same spot in your local newspaper, will attract the reader to look for them, giving a reason to visit your place of business.

BUILDING A REPUTATION

Honesty must be first and foremost in anything you do. You want to be trusted and continue selling. You have to figure out first what you want to achieve. How much money do you have available? Do not be fooled by the so-called notion that you cannot grow without advertising.

This is not true at all. If you have a unique product, it is well-priced and of wonderful quality, the word gets around. Many business owners go shopping and they see what is being offered and ask questions. Stores recommend successful products to other stores in different areas. All this is not immediate, but in time you will reap results.

Meanwhile, you will be able to streamline your operation and be ready to grow on a firm dependable basis. You build a wonderful reputation. That is what you want when you start in business, whether you have a store, a service company, whatever.

Of course, you never have enough business. You constantly have to be out there looking for other customers, refining and improving your product line and your service. I find that by being loyal to the customers you do have and giving them the best service you can, you will make your business more successful and enjoyable.

IMAGE

It takes a long time to create the image of your company. This is the most important and long-lasting impression you want to make. This, of course, is created by the way you handle your business, the service you give your customers, the way you protect territories without having customers make that request, and the consistent quality of your product or service. Developing your image first allows you to stay longer in the market, and second, you may even be able to demand a higher price for your goods and services because of your image.

> **A business grows only with the strictest integrity.**

Identifying your product usually costs a lot in creating an image with your logo and name, but when you start your own business you do not have access to unlimited amounts of money. Therefore, you create your image by acting the way I described, and you will reach your goals on a sure foot in time.

A business grows only with the strictest integrity. With integrity you will get referrals and the word spreads; this is so much better than advertising. Never embellish your product or service to a degree where you can-

IMAGE

not deliver on promises. It will only come back to hurt you. Whatever new and extra features you offer should be enough. Exaggeration is a trap.

Any company once established needs to invest time and energy to try different methods, to find out how to improve their products and create some new ones. This has to be done very slowly and only by testing the market before making costly mistakes. It is essential to improve your product, find ways to best utilize your time, and manage production costs. Adding a new product will produce additional income with minimal additional efforts.

I am speaking from experience. When I ventured into new products, even sizes, some of them proved to be failures and I lost money. I constantly reviewed our sales, and whenever I spotted a product that was not selling well, I discontinued it. I kept only the best sellers.

IMAGE

a story...

I specialized and improved every year. One year I felt my envelopes needed upgrading, so we lined them. I did not hear anyone complimenting me for bettering my product, so I asked one of our clients. Her answer was, "We probably thought that if we expressed our approval, you might increase your price."

In marketing you must be innovative and unique. Even if you copy someone's idea, try to give it your own slant. With practice you will be able to achieve that special way of being recognized.

When I started painting, I kept coming out with new ideas and always thought I had something different. Yet, after finishing the image, it looked so similar to the ones I did before, it disturbed me so much until I realized I have a definite style and look. There may be copies, but my work is still readily identified. It was a good thing though it distressed me at the time to have all that effort and hard work turn out looking so similar.

IMAGE

a story...

Several times I wanted to try new approaches and failed. I was definitely identified with a certain look. One of my clients told me the following story.

One of their suppliers had a line of products that appealed to her customers very much. It consistently sold extremely well. They carried the same line for years and years. This supplier became tired and decided to change her image and create a new look. Sales just stopped. When my good friend and client told me that story, she meant for me to learn that it is very difficult to change your look.

There is nothing wrong with finding a niche with a particular clientele. The trick is to keep this look going, improving in quality and design every time.

PRICING

The old saying is true: Price is what someone is willing to pay. Competing in the business world on price alone is never advisable. There will always be someone else who will undercut you in price. You must have a definite new approach, a new twist, something that distinguishes you from everyone else. Find it and you are way ahead of the crowd.

The worst thing you can do is oversell.

The worst thing you can do is oversell, especially to smaller outlets who do not have the volume necessary to overstock on any one item. They need variety. Always ask yourself the question they need to be asking before they buy: "What and how much would I like to buy for my volume of sales?"

MARKETING

PRICING

a story...

This invaluable lesson I learned while attending a craft show in San Francisco. Next to me were a couple of young men offering their product. They were consistently busy selling. Their product was a clay image of a cowboy with a rope around his neck, the hanging cowboy.

We started talking and they told me their experience in pricing. They took this product to market and priced it at $25 each. Sales were slow and few. So they lowered their price to $10 and again sales did not improve. Then they decided to sell them at $18 each and bingo, a huge success.

They were able to do this because they had nothing printed, so they could test the market. This is the best way. The price of any item is not what it cost you to produce, or the time it took you to create it. It is *only what the customer is willing to pay*.

PRICING

a story...

One of our most successful items is an enclosure card; we call it our "fold-over card." All of these years we have sold quantities of these little cards.

When I was a novice, my salespeople suggested that I had no idea of how to sell them. They said I should do what everyone else did, sell them in a pre-packaged box assorted in quantities of 24 dozen. This way they said sales volume would increase.

I never followed their advice because, as usual, I put myself in the position of a store owner. Why would I put so much money in a product where perhaps 3 of the 24 designs sold fast and well, but in order to get these three you have to order again a full assortment?

Besides, 24 dozen was too much for a small store. They want variety. I have been proven right. The fold-over card is one of our best-selling sizes, and we keep reprinting them all the time. Our customers pick and choose.

PRICING

a story...

While visiting Rio de Janeiro, I found one of the most original marketing ideas. I visited one of the boutiques where I found an extremely beautiful dress and asked whether they had my size. The saleslady told me to try it on. I did and noticed that she was pulling the dress on the back until it fit my figure. You see, she had only one size and she fitted these dresses to the client.

I had to return for a second fitting. While being fitted, I was shown some other dresses and I purchased another one. What a wonderful way to sell! No big inventory of expensive dresses in different sizes. Plus, we women do not want to know our size—we usually claim a smaller one! By fitting these dresses they seemed made-to-order and tailored for the client. Great idea, probably learned by listening to their customers. By the way, there was no charge for alterations; they were included in the price.

Another wonderful marketing idea: I know of a firm that started very small, selling sport clothes. The clothes are quite attractive and the

PRICING

firm changes their look almost daily. Now the big marketing idea again is to fit these sport clothes, shorten them, or take them in as needed. Again, no charge and they are ready overnight. Such a success! They started with one store and now have 14.

LISTEN TO YOUR CUSTOMERS

The success of a company I am familiar with was due to the owner listening to her customers. She followed the wishes of one of her clients and manufactured a particular product. Because the minimums, especially in printing, are so large, she overproduced and had to take the excess of this new product to market. Guess what? That was 10 years ago, and she is still the leader in a huge market today with that particular product.

Personalize your relations with your clients.

Accept criticism by listening to what your customers tell you. Any problem that needs your attention, correct it immediately. For any suggestions of new products or improvements, do research on these new ideas and take action if you feel there may be an opportunity. Our best product was a suggestion by a client who told me to use the whole sheet of paper by printing a small card.

Personalize your relations with your clients. This suggestion refers mostly to professionals. There is nothing more irritating than visiting your doctor, dentist, etc., and they do not even remember who you are. Why not write on the patient's chart a little note telling some-

LISTEN TO YOUR CUSTOMERS

thing personal about the patient? How much more effective to walk in and have the professional man or woman open your chart and ask you a short personal question that would put you at ease. It would also further your continuing relationship and support.

Always treat your clients as though they are the most important people to you because they are! Honesty and integrity will mark your business, and your reputation must be cultivated, cherished and watched at all times. Place your clients' concerns at the top of your list—if you are loyal to them, they will be loyal to you.

In our business our policy is the old saying, "The customer is always right." If they claim shortages, we do not question this and immediately replace whatever they ask. The only thing we do is mark this claim in the computer, and if a shortage is claimed again, we will replace the items, but when a third one occurs, we then stop selling to that company.

LISTEN TO YOUR CUSTOMERS

a story...

One of the top central buyers of a large furniture chain once told me, "When I buy accessories of art pieces, I purchase them in small quantities, yet when I purchase sofas, chairs, etc., I place orders in the hundreds of units."

It all depends on what products have mass appeal. Make sure you understand the role of buyer and seller. Each one is looking out for their own interests. The buyer wants to get the most for his money. He must like what he purchases and is willing to pay for it in the quantities his experience taught him. The seller is interested mainly in converting his product into money with the expectation that he will sell several times more to this entity, generating profits.

LISTEN TO YOUR CUSTOMERS

a story...

Another buyer at a very large department store that is middle of the road in price told me that when she was viewing a line that appealed to her personally, she did not purchase that product. She knew her taste was with top-of-the-line, high-priced boutiques, or department stores that cater to exclusive clientele. She had to keep her job and knew what sold in her stores.

LISTEN TO YOUR CUSTOMERS

a story...

One buyer told me she never brought back last year's tremendous success. She wanted something new. There is a reason for this. Usually stores located in medium or small cities have their steady clientele who visit their stores frequently and they want something new. If they bought a particular item last year and wanted another house gift, it had to be different. We are always on the lookout for something "new."

New is the key word in sales.

SALES REPRESENTATIVES

Sales representatives are people with different aptitudes. They are not good as managers. They are independent people who like it just fine the way it is for them. They work their own hours and days. They do not want anyone to regulate or be constantly on top of them telling them what to do. The only things they are interested in are 1) having a product that sells and 2) being paid their commissions promptly and accurately.

When hiring sales representatives you will find it a hit and miss operation.

Sales representatives are particular about what companies they want to represent. After all, they must sell a product to their client that "checks out" (in the trade talk for one that sells well). They do not want to push a "dawg" (a product that does not retail well). They have to make sure that the next time they call on their clients they will be welcomed.

When hiring sales representatives, you will find it is a hit and miss operation, and it takes time to develop a sales organization. Experience taught me the best ways to contract salespeople are:

SALES REPRESENTATIVES

1) Call your best clients in a particular area and ask them to suggest a sales representative. They will recommend someone who carries products related to yours. You can rightly assume this person calls on prospective clients in your specific "niche."

2) When they call you directly and want to carry your line. This means they have seen your product and checked with the store and found out that these items indeed sell very well. They want it!

SALES REPRESENTATIVES

a story...

One of the best designers of cards has a most beautiful and unusual line. My salespeople who sometimes have also carried her product commented to me that it took them hours to fill an order. She had so many choices in colors and finishes and when at last they finished with the order taking, most of the items were back-ordered. She manufactured only on demand, but that demand varied so that she could not carry inventory.

The buyers at the end of this long process forgot what they ordered or when it arrived were disappointed in their choice. Keep in mind one color, one image—simplify, simplify.

After all, your salespeople need to go in and out fast. After they write up an order, they have to move to their next appointment. When writing up an order that is too tedious and takes a long time, they lose money. Simplify your price list and choices. Copy from other successful companies.

THE BEST SALESPERSON

The best salesperson is the one who has the best product at the best price. The mistaken idea is that a great talker is the best salesperson. My experience is that if you talk a customer into something, you have not made a FIRM SALE.

I prefer the system of contacting the person in charge of purchasing and showing them your product. That person is extremely versed in your kind of product. He/she has other similar items in the store. Let him/her look it over. Once you've been asked questions, and if your price is competitive and your product has merit, then it is a FIRM SALE. If you talk too much, the buyers resent it. They want to make up their own minds.

If you talk too much, the buyers resent it.

When you contact a store, first decide whether they carry items similar to yours. You want competition. You will do so much better when there are other products in the same line because this means they have developed a clientele for these items. Regardless of what people think, I believe in competition. Let the best item win.

THE BEST SALESPERSON

If a particular party is not responsive to you the first time, you may try them again. But I definitely do not believe in fast talkers or pushy sales pitches. You must gain the buyer's trust, and that is obtained solely on the relationship you develop with them.

THE BEST SALESPERSON

a story...

I met a young man at a trade show with an innovative, wonderful product that I was sure would be a great success. I ran into him again a year or so later and asked him what happened. He told me that he had engaged a salesperson to offer his product who told him that he found it did not have the acceptance required. He then dropped the project.

There is nothing wrong with salespeople. They, like every one of us, have their own interest at heart. If a product is not accepted readily, they do not want to lose their time recommending something that is new and has not proven to be a successful item. If they force a new product on their clients, and the new one is not a good seller, they may lose that account.

My friend from the trade show would have been so much better off if he personally had gone out and visited his prospective clients. He would not have given up with one or two rejections. It was HIS PRODUCT and he had to go on regardless, until he found his NICHE. He would have learned at the same time a lot

THE BEST SALESPERSON

of other important information that only he could evaluate and profit from—knowledge that is so valuable, but his salespeople would not have hit upon it.

WHY USE SALES REPS?

You must realize that the more outlets you have for your product, the more sales you will have. With only you selling, you do retain 100% of your profit, but how many orders can you get?

The best business is a wholesale business. My father taught me this. We had a very large mill that employed hundreds of people, and we mass marketed. He felt better selling to more businesses rather than having one store. With wholesale you have many stores to sell to; with retail you have one chance, your own. We are blessed here in the U.S. to have 51 states and so many stores.

To understand the advantages of using salespeople, let's look at the sale of Widget X for a hypothetical business:

WHY USE SALES REPS?

SELLING "WIDGET X" PERSONALLY

Retail price of Widget X(assuming you multiply cost by 5 which is the number most businesses use):

	$1.25
Cost of widget	$0.25
Gross profit	1.00
Less travel, food, time	0.10
Profit before other expenses	$0.90

Assume you average 3 sales per day for 5 days = 60 sales a month (15 x 4 weeks = 60). Your profit would be 60 x .90 = $54.

SELLING THROUGH SALESPEOPLE

Retail price	$1.25
Discount to retailer (50% off…retailer will "keystone")	.625
10% commission	.125
Cost of widget	.25
Total cost:	$1.00 per Widget X
Profit before other expenses	$.25 per Widget X

WHY USE SALES REPS?

Now, assume you have 10 representatives selling your product, and each one of them sells 40 widgets a month (please note I only averaged for each just 40 sales per month). Your profit would be 40 x .25 x 10 salespeople = $100.

These numbers can be changed in a number of ways. Less or more commissions, lower cost of product when manufacturing larger quantities, etc. When I used "40 sales a month" above, that was assuming that the salesperson would have other products to sell and would not assign all his/her time to your product, while you would only concentrate on yours.

Keep multiplying this by more and more salespeople and you can see the advantage of employing salespeople. This will free your time to manage your business, create other things, and visit with in-house clients.

You may ask, why is this important to understand? Many people think it is not fair to discount 50% to the buyer while you spent all this time and money creating this product and not netting even the same amount. This misconception is very detrimental.

THE "TRAVELING SALESMAN"

Necessity is the mother of invention. This adage is perfectly suitable to a great idea we've come up with, "The Traveling Salesman." This single idea is worth more than what you paid for this book!

We understand that salespeople sometimes get tired after many years of carrying the same line. They want something new. Or, they may only have one account in a certain area that buys your product; they may not want to travel many miles for just one order.

This single idea is worth more than what you paid for this book.

We refrain from contacting clients who are being serviced by our sales representatives. We value our relationship with them very much. They are our lifeblood, but we must also protect our clients and service those who have been neglected.

For their own personal reasons, some of our salespeople were not covering their territories. Their sales diminished to a trickle. We would find this out when our clients repeatedly called us directly. We contacted our salespeople with this information, but no action

THE "TRAVELING SALESMAN"

was taken. We had to do something. Our solution was "The Traveling Salesman," a full sales kit sent directly to the customer.

We pride ourselves on service. The following proved extremely successful. It will require you to create a new routine. After many trials and errors, this is the sequence of events we follow.

SETTING UP THE SALESMAN

Nowadays when we receive a request for our catalog we send them the Traveling Salesman kit. The ratio of new orders is so superior to mailing "just a catalog."

1. Type a form:

Name _____

Account # _____ Date Contacted _____

Address _____

City, State, Zip _____

Attn: _____

Telephone _____

2. Phone your established account, ask for the person who does the purchasing. Identify yourself. "We are checking with our customers to find out whether you need to reorder our product and to let you know of our new service. We mail you a kit with all the up-to-date samples for you to look at. Within 10 days we either call you again, or you let us know when we can order UPS to pick up this kit. It does not cost you anything. You can reorder this service anytime you want to review our line before placing another order."

SETTING UP THE SALESMAN

3. We fill out the form and file it in alphabetical order in its own folder.
4. We print a label and ship it out. (On the filled form we attach the UPS label.)

The kit consists of the following:

1) A hard plastic container (we use ones that are sold as home filing boxes).
2) Samples of our products.
3) Two order blanks.
4) A list of contents, including a catalog of our products.
5) On the cover of the kit we place printed instructions for our clients to: "Please save the cardboard box for its return trip." These cardboard boxes are thrown away and replaced with fresh ones every time we ship them again.
6) A printed memo with remarks sent us from satisfied clients. *(See comments following.)*
7) We again contact our clients to order UPS to pick them up. Working from our filed first sheet, we list the date when we ordered the pick-up, filing this sheet, this time in another alphabetized folder.

SETTING UP THE SALESMAN

8) When the kits return, we review them and fill them up again.

9) Usually an order may be enclosed, faxed or phoned in. If this is not the case, we again file the printed sheet to follow up within two weeks and ask when they are placing their order. If an order is placed, we throw away this sheet.

Of course, it took lots of money and time preparing these kits. Add to this the cost of shipping and picking them up. But the results have been astounding. You may have to have someone in your office keep track of all these procedures.

This system did not start like this. It evolved like everything else, improving procedures every time. Before adding the UPS pick-up, which saves our clients trips to mail or ship back these kits, we found some resistance. The minute we implemented the pick-ups, it worked like a charm. After a year with this system we now constantly get calls asking for the kit.

One of our employees suggested that we enclose a little gift from our company as "compliments of [your company]" for trying the Traveling Salesman. We always listen to suggestions from our people and follow them.

SETTING UP THE SALESMAN

From satisfied customers...

• He was great! Low key, laid back and non-aggressive.

• We love your Traveling Salesman—least pushy man we've ever dealt with!

• It was great seeing all the products at one time, especially in our time, at our pace. Great way to sell!

• I like your idea of the Traveling Salesbox a lot. I was able to order at my leisure and think you will be very successful with this approach.

• Our time is valuable…this makes ordering so easy!

• Your salesman is ready to go home! He's the only salesman who works in your living room at 10 p.m.!

• I have the martinis ready for the next visit.

• I liked the salesman so well that I took him out to lunch. Here I am helping him choose his entrée. In the other photo he and I are bonding.

Rozy's Rules
Three Keys To Success

1
You must have a product that sells!

2
You must charge enough for your product or service to generate a profit.

3
**Management:
You must be organized.
It's your business...you must know what's going on.**

NOTES:

Management
(Organization)

GETTING ORGANIZED
Practical, proven business practices for small business owners...not theory!

Organization is so important. Suppose you have a product, people want it, but within one year in business, you've lost it. You owe money. You are constantly worried about what to do to pay your bills. WHY? You had a wonderful product that sold well in stores. What caused this mess?

There are three ways to mess up your business:

1. Lack of organization.
2. Overcharging
3. Undercharging.

You may ask how overcharging causes a loss in your business. The reason is simple: By overcharging you can only sell to a select few and you limit your market. With undercharging, by trying to become competitive, you lower your margin of profit to a dangerous level, with no margin left for mistakes.

Following are a number of specific ideas on ORGANIZATION, beginning with Banking–Money Matters, and continuing with other suggestions learned after so many years in business.

GETTING ORGANIZED

a story...

I will never forget when I attended a lecture of Lin Yu Tang, a famous philosopher and writer. I enjoyed so much his commentaries, I mentioned to my friend who was with me how wonderful it was to have had the opportunity to listen to him personally after reading his books.

My friend said she did not enjoy it because "Everyone can understand it." In order to enjoy something, she felt it had to be so difficult that very few people could understand what was said, and they must use a language so contrived that very few comprehend what is said and done.

My idea is different. I prefer simplicity, common language, so that everyone can understand what was said and done. Simplification is my motto. Make whatever you do or sell accessible to everyone.

TIME MANAGEMENT ROUTINES

Developing a habit of routines is extremely valuable. It means that you take care of daily pesky little matters and can free your mind of the pressure "TO DO" things, to clear clutters of paper on your desk, schedule appointments, make telephone calls. Your mind will then be free to think clearly and attend to creative matters that will result in profits. You will know you are up-to-date.

Following are some basic routines I've found useful through the years.

GREETING AND MEETING WITH PERSONNEL

Meet daily with your secretary, bookkeeper, staff, preferably on a one-to-one basis. This way you can check what everyone is doing that day and ask them what problems need to be taken care of.

Schedule workload, shipments, collection calls, follow-up calls, etc. In general, show them you are in command and your whole staff will understand this.

GREETING AND MEETING PERSONNEL

a story...

Many years ago I wanted to take it somewhat easier, so I delegated many of these functions to an employee who wanted to become a supervisor. We employed at that time 10-12 people.

We had moved out of our home after three years working out of the garage in our home. We rented a different place for our business. Since I still did much of my work at home, I visited this new place every other day for a few hours. I soon saw that things were not the way they were supposed to be. I discussed these matters with my 'supervisor," and yet when I returned next time nothing was done. After three times of making the same observations, I became mad and told her so, and left for my home.

Upon entering my home the phone was ringing. My "supervisor" was requesting me to meet with her and the rest of the crew at a restaurant to discuss their grievances…to come right away! I told her I did not think they had any reason to be upset; besides I had an appointment with a supplier and did not have

GREETING AND MEETING PERSONNEL

time for that. She then told me, "If that is the case, we will all quit working for you." My answer was, "Go ahead." As a boss you can never allow anyone to intimidate you. That meant the loss of 12 employees, my whole crew.

I proceeded to call several of the employees who I knew needed the job and paycheck very badly. I found out that they were going to go with her since she was their supervisor. This incident happened on a weekend. Monday morning I came in early and locked myself in my shop with a big sign saying, "Workers needed." The former employees came en masse and stayed outside for some time until they finally left. It has always been my policy never to argue. *Just take action.*

This was an extremely hard and painful lesson. I found out that by her handing over their paychecks, she had somehow given the impression that this was her business. I learned later from the employment office, where they all went to claim benefits, that they were reprimanded, especially the so-called supervisor.

GREETING AND MEETING PERSONNEL

They were refused any benefits. The man at the employment office called me to say he was absolutely astounded at what one woman could do.

That meant that me, my husband and a friend of ours started to work in the plant. My hours were from 4:00 a.m. on. I missed having my previous employees who used to help new ones and show them what to do. But after one week, I had a new crew and we were shipping out orders.

From that day on I made it a point to check with every one of my employees daily. It takes only a few minutes. This does not mean you become their best friend or they confide in you. But it makes them feel important and they will share their valuable suggestions knowing you are there to listen to them.

OPEN MAIL

You may want to be the one to keep track of all mail received. You will learn about problems, complaints, compliments or whatever crosses your desk.

OPEN MAIL

a story...

I once received a duplicate check for an order for a very large amount. I knew someone in that company was not up to snuff. I called the company and asked to talk to the owner. I informed him that I was returning his check.

The envelope was addressed to him personally. I called him because I felt he as well as I would personally like to know about a mistake of this size. He was so grateful. He is still buying from us.

Mistakes can be made by yourself or the best of your employees, but you do want to know about them. You want to be informed about everything, including problems. You do not want surprises or anyone to cover someone else's actions.

CLEANING UP

This sounds like such an elementary suggestion. Believe me, if you have your employees take a few minutes daily to leave their stations in order and clean up, productivity increases.

Upon entering a place of business, if you see a mess and no rhyme or reason why cartons and boxes are all over, work benches or desks messed up, you will know that this company needs some organization. You get a sense of whether a business is successful or not by just entering their premises.

MONEY MATTERS: BASIC TIPS

❶ *A business owner must be frugal and methodical with money.*

❷ *The owner must be the last to draw money from the business. His suppliers and employees come first.*

❸ *By not owing money you save. Save 2% by paying within terms on all your bills and taking discounts.*

❹ *If you take care of the small expenses, the big ones will take care of themselves.*

❺ *If you cannot pay suppliers, call and let them know when you will pay.*

❻ *Have a definite system for collections.*

MONEY MATTERS

Money is a key issue for a successful business—the most important matter. Any other area or chore you can eventually delegate, but money matters must be taken care of by YOU. If you take care of money matters yourself, you will have the assurance that any mistakes are yours and only yours, no need to figure out what went wrong, who did what, or who took what.

THIS IS A MUST! I cannot stress this enough. You never have to wonder whether any of your employees can or cannot be trusted. So many things can happen in your business, but at least with this question removed as a possible problem, what a terrific relief! If you have your doubts about this suggestion, read the newspapers and see how many horror stories there are about loss of monies in small and large businesses.

> **Money matters must be taken care of by you.**

A friend of mine mentioned that someone in our area, a very successful business person, was invited to lecture to a business class about suggestions and experiences. She took notes and told me that whatever we talked about in this book was exactly what this very

MONEY MATTERS

prosperous person talked about. Of course, being the business owner, she was most emphatically suggesting control of Money Matters. There are very simple procedures that we all follow in order to succeed and survive in business.

Control of money is vital to your company. It is the lifeblood that runs your company.

Though it may seem like no job is delegated when I write the checks and make the deposits, all these banking procedures help me know exactly where I stand in money matters. Control of money is vital to your company. It is the lifeblood that runs your company. I repeat myself once more: by having only one person writing checks and making deposits, only one person is responsible.

MONEY MATTERS

a story...

I once hired a bookkeeper who after a month told me, "Why keep me if you write the checks, make the deposits, and keep track of accounts receivables and accounts payable?"

OUT SHE WENT!

YOUR CHECKING ACCOUNT

Most people think writing checks is where someone can play tricks with your money. True to a degree. The largest risk is in deposits. The new computer programs make it easy for you to write your checks fast and accurately, therefore you have a reliable paper trail. You have a record.

Always pay by check. Keep no cash on the premises, just a small petty cash fund for immediate expenses. All bills should be paid from your home. Pay only from invoices which you then stamp PAID. You can then turn over these documents to the bookkeeper to be filed.

DEPOSITS

We list our deposits by date, invoice number, client name and amount. Every order is then stamped "paid" with a stamp that automatically writes paid with the date of the deposit. When stamping the paid invoices, we remove the colored strips that have been flagged when a statement was mailed. We then throw away the copy of the statement we used for collection calls.

A copy of every deposit list is filed with its consecutive deposit number.

DEPOSITS

a story...

I learned the hard way about the value of deposits. Many years ago I owned and operated a travel agency.

On one occasion I went away on a trip and left one of my daughters in charge. She came daily and took care of the deposits. I had implemented a system listing on the back of the deposit slip: 1) invoice number; 2) name of client; 3) amount paid.

I would personally stamp PAID on all the invoices which I kept in a locked drawer in my desk. I would then hand over the checks, cash, and the deposit slip to my secretary to fill in and send to the bank. We did quite a large cash business.

When I returned my daughter asked me, "Mother, do you realize that funds are being stolen from you?" How could this happen? I was sure my system was foolproof. By delegating the deposits to my daughter, she began adding the back of the deposit slip and matched it to the front where my secretary had filled in the amount. The amounts did not match. I had missed this important step!

DEPOSITS

a story...

While visiting a relative of mine in his office, his accountant walked in with some papers. My relative excused himself, picked up the papers, and opened his locked drawer and took out a list. He then used a ruler and a red pencil. I did not have to ask him what he was doing. He was checking that the amounts deposited matched against his list of outstanding invoices. His business, though very large, sold to distributors only. Therefore his invoices were not as many as mine, yet he took care of double checking himself. He was doing a volume in the millions every month.

———

CREDIT APPLICATIONS

We disregard credit references. People give only their best references. What we look for in their credit applications are the names of companies they do business with. By knowing from whom they buy, I can better determine what kind of business it is.

ORDER PROCESSING

The first response after receiving an order is, "Great, I need sales!" But it is so much better to be judicious to avoid future problems. Depending on your volume, processing orders should take one-half hour or less. When you have a good computer program, it will take less time. YOU MUST check what the status of a customer is.

The judgment depends on you alone. If they have an outstanding balance, you remind them that when a check arrives, the merchandise will be shipped.

COLLECTIONS

Special note: 85% of our accounts pay within terms, i.e. 30 days net. Here again is a system we developed after years of trial and error. It is extremely simple.

Employing a collection agency does not work well at all. You have to pay them 50% or thereabouts for amounts collected. Then the law does not allow them to make more than a certain number of telephone calls. So they simply mail a lawyerly letter demanding payment. Clients do not pay too much attention to these form letters. They simply disregard them.

Employing a collection agency does not work that well at all.

However, as business owners, WE CAN TELEPHONE ABOUT COLLECTIONS AS OFTEN AS NEEDED.

My collection system is the following:

- Our terms are 30 days net. On small orders we enclose the original invoice with the order, usually when orders are purchased and shipped to the same address.

- After 30 days we mail a statement. This means that every week we mail statements to different accounts.

COLLECTIONS

- Two weeks after mailing this statement, we make our first call...just a reminder that their bill is outstanding.
- We wait another two weeks before calling again. By then their bill is 60 days overdue.
- If payment has not been received one week later, someone else calls again. This time we repeat the intensity of calls until they finally pay their bill. We keep this system going all the time.

The paperwork required for this follow-up is minimal. Our printed statements consist of two copies; one goes to the client with its own pre-addressed envelope. The second copy we keep and use for follow-up.

For each statement mailed, we use colored strips of paper to flag the invoice, writing on these strips the account and invoice number. We then insert these strips in our consecutive file. Each week we use a different color. A card listing when to make the first, second call, etc. is attached to the copies of all statements mailed that week. On the back of our copy we write any notes, date called, whom we spoke to and their reply.

The colored strips make it easier to spot invoices paid when we stamp them after depositing their check. We

COLLECTIONS

then proceed to throw away the statement copy which we used as a follow-up.

REMEMBER: If they are not prompt payers, it does not matter what you do. They will probably go out of business. (This applies only between business to business, not business to consumer.) You can call every day if you want to. Be persistent. Keep asking for payment.

COLLECTIONS

a story...

Some time ago while waiting for my plane after a New York trade show, I chatted with a young man who had also attended the show. He asked me what I did to obtain loans from the bank. He said that the first thing he had to do upon his return was go to his bank and request a loan to pay commissions and obtain new working capital. "I use my inventory as collateral," he said.

I asked him, knowing well what his answers would be, "How large an inventory do you have? How many references (products on hand) do you have? How large is your accounts receivables?" His answer was: Too large an inventory, too many references, and a very large accounts receivable.

If he would watch whom to ship to, do his statements, and follow-up his accounts receivables and limit his references to best sellers, he would definitely be in better shape. By having so many items in his inventory, his profits were on his shelves. By not paying attention to accounts receivables, there was too much money outstanding waiting to be collected.

COLLECTIONS

There is no need for so many references. Regardless of how many you have, your clients know how much money they want to spend on your line. By limiting their options to only the best-sellers, order taking will be so much easier and quicker and less capital will be tied up in inventory.

CASH ON DELIVERY

We discourage C.O.D. We do C.O.D. only when established customers request it. Many companies are doing this now. Instead of C.O.D., we offer free freight for any new order prepaid over a certain amount.

Usually, when selling during a trade show, your clients order C.O.D., anticipating that by the time the order will arrive, they will have the money. When the order comes they can refuse to accept it. By then you are losing: a) freight and C.O.D. charges; b) handling the order, c) accounting and invoice printing costs.

C.O.D.'S

a story...

Here is an expensive lesson we learned about C.O.D. Unfortunately it is quite a common practice. When the order is C.O.D. and requires several cartons, you must apply the C.O.D. sticker to each and every box. By trying to save extra charges to our customer, we would put a C.O.D. tag only on box #1. What happened was that the client accepted all subsequent cartons, but not box #1.

Expensive lesson learned!

PROFIT & LOSS STATEMENTS

Understanding and simplifying profit and loss statements is frequently a question students ask in business classes. We need to know how much we actually have and what we need to meet our obligations.

A long time ago one of my excellent CPA's taught me the simplest method. At the end of every month I take a sheet of paper and divide it into three columns. For example:

(1) + Monies On Hand	(2) − Break-even Expenses	(3) − Monies Owed
($) Bank	Rent	Company WWW
($) Accts. Receivables	Telephone	Company XXX
	Salaries	Company YYY
Total $1,000.00	Taxes	Company ZZZ
	Transportation	Total $300.00
	Total $200.00	

Column 1 lists cash in bank plus accounts receivables. **Column 2** lists fixed expenses, like rent, salaries, taxes, telephone, etc. **Column 3** lists outstanding bills to be paid.

Add Column (2) and (3) = $500.00.
Column (1) less Columns (2) and (3) = $500.00.
Subtract 10-20% for unforeseen additional expenses ($100.00).

PROFIT & LOSS STATEMENTS

The result is a total of $400 left over as profit.

The additional 10-20% has to be added for unforeseen expenses, a security measure.

Add Columns 1 and 2 and subtract Column 3 and the 10-20% for unforeseen expenses. Now you know how much money you are left with every month.

UNFORSEEN EXTRAS: Believe me, you need to add this margin for security purposes. Do not be fooled thinking you will not spend anything more than what you list. Another reason to be on top of your Accounts Receivables. Other expenses always pop up, so be prepared.

This little exercise done every month will show you all you need to know. Your major accounting is then done by your bookkeeper. Later on, when your business has grown you may want to learn to use the excellent computer accounting programs available, but I leave this to my staff. For myself, my sheet of paper is all I want and need to know.

Is it absolutely essential to learn the intricacies of accounting? NO! Something simplified is the answer. My system works.

HIRING EMPLOYEES

How do you find good employees? This is another frequently-asked question. I find it is a hit-and-miss proposition. I rely on my instincts and prefer a personal interview.

Here are some hints on what I have found works:

- We never check references. They only give people who will say positive things.
- They have to be "hungry to work," "I need a job." If they ask, "What are your benefits?" don't hire.
- If someone asks, "What are you going to pay me?" do not hire. YOU are the one who asks, "What were you making before you applied for this job?" You are in command and decide what amount you decide this job warrants. If they are interested only in money, they will be hopping from one job to another.
- They must be neat, no airs. We don't have room for prima donnas.
- We have no written job descriptions. You do not want to limit yourself. Yours is a small business. You may need them to fill in on different jobs for a day or hours, and you do not want them to answer, "This is not in my job description."

HIRING EMPLOYEES

- Everyone should be trained to do multiple jobs, to change from job to job. It is the best way—cross training—because they can replace absentee employees. It is to their benefit since they gain more experience.
- We always pay more than the market does. We do not want job hoppers.
- All of the formatted job applications give you information, but you had better check with them personally. Lately, I have experienced hiring people who claimed in their printed resumes that they were acquainted with and used numerous computer programs, but several of them did not even know how to turn a computer on and off!

TRAINING EMPLOYEES

Some jobs require more training and time to learn the procedures and ways of a company, especially today with the use of computers. For those jobs, we allow time for the new person to spend learning on-the-job and becoming productive. Bookkeeping, special printing jobs, and shipping need more time. For the jobs we have that do not require special experience, our procedure for training is very simple:

> **On-the-job learning is the best and fastest way.**

- A new employee has to **watch** their counterparts the first day. No talking or asking questions. No manuals to read, nothing. Just watch.

- The second day the new employee can ask questions and do simple chores.

- They learn on the job. They are able to do everything.

- Within five working days, they are rolling along, fully productive.

- If they find a better way to do the job, let them try it.

TRAINING EMPLOYEES

My reason for the new employee not talking or asking questions is: Once they see someone else do that job, no matter how difficult it looks at first, they figure out, "If she or he can do it, I will be able to do it too." Learning by reading is best as a reference, a form of asking questions. On-the-job learning is the best and fastest way.

TRAINING EMPLOYEES

a story...

I recall when I learned to drive a car. I was so tense and scared that I would hurt someone. I took driving classes and still was shy of driving. One day I saw the mother of a friend of mine driving a car. She was a very short lady and quite old. I then told myself, "If she can do it, I can too!"

TRAINING EMPLOYEES

a story...

My mother had a wonderful system when I was growing up. We employed servants, and when a new person came to work, she asked them to clean and wash everything in the kitchen, even though she had a spotless kitchen. I asked Mother, "Why waste their time cleaning when everything is already spotless?" Her answer was: "This way I will not have to point out to them where everything is. They will know where things are. They cleaned the place."

THE MOST IMPORTANT PERSON

Yes, you depend on your employees to keep your business going. But what would happen to your business if you were no longer managing it? It is true that the employees are excellent and best in their respective jobs. If you had to replace them on those particular jobs, you would not be as effective as they are. You would need to do the same job daily to acquire their skills.

Still—you are the most important person in your business. YOU DESERVE ALL OF THE MONEY YOU CAN EARN. You are the one who holds the strings of all the marionettes and make them perform. You are the one who is taking all the economic risks. YOU DESERVE THE REWARDS. You do not go home after a day's work and simply forget about everything. You live and breathe your business.

You deserve all of the money you can earn.

Do not keep an employee who claims, "Without me the business is nothing." If people look at orders or revenues coming in, they think they are responsible for the company's growth. You know they are only looking at the trees—they don't see the forest. They do not see all the expenses. They are not risking anything. They do not know the whole picture.

EXPECTATIONS OF EMPLOYEES

Number one: Employees should do their work. Do not get personal with your employees. You do not want to know their aches and pains, and they are not going to know yours. You are not going to be pals. This does change when they work with you for many years, however. Time makes you become closer to your employees whom you have learned to trust.

By your knowledge and experience of having performed every phase of the business, you will realize faster who is working and who is just killing time, which is what you want to avoid. This tendency is contagious in a workplace, and you want your employees to follow the example of conscientious workers rather than the ones who fake work.

Start layering your company with people you trust to whom you can delegate responsibility. This will take time.

EMPLOYEE RELATIONS

Try to have your employees first take pride in the company. Have them feel a sense of accomplishment by watching the growth of the company where they have had some degree of input into it. They will feel proud of where they work. They respect it when there are no collection calls and your finances are under control. Their paycheck is always on time. Commissions are paid on schedule. The company is growing and they want to continue working there because they feel they will be rewarded with a better salary or position within the company.

Do not give titles to your employees.

Do not give titles to your employees. Everyone works on their respective job. You do not want them to become subjected to someone else who tries to lord over other employees. If you have someone that you notice wants to become a "supervisor" and complains to you about how no one is any good—only them—get rid of them really fast!

Build a team!

EMPLOYEE RELATIONS

a story...

I once had a very capable employee who constantly called me at home after hours to complain about the other employees. She was really excellent, and it took me a long time to realize what she was all about. We had a small crew of people, and I knew it would take a few weeks for a new person to fit in. Yet, she wanted me to fire a new person only after two or three days. She felt threatened by them being efficient. When she left, everything fell into place. I had to learn that lesson which cost me a lot of aggravation. So I suggest to you to watch out for people like that.

MORE ABOUT EMPLOYEES

All your business dealings must be an open book. Do not forget that all employees know exactly what goes on. They may appear not to notice things, but believe me, they do. Every shipment must have an invoice. There are no two different accounting books. Do you want to have a disgruntled employee go to the IRS? Always be above board on all your business dealings. Always know that anything you do which is not correct will eventually catch up with you.

Always be above board on all business dealings.

I once asked my bookkeeper what I did differently than she had experienced in the past when she worked in other businesses, and she answered, "You know everything that is going on here."

A major problem today is absenteeism. If you encounter it, try all the old-fashioned ways to deal with it. Fire the employee if he or she persists. Obviously, you cannot possibly operate a business with no people when you need them. Or, simply pay them by the hour; this way they lose pay if they don't work. Whichever way you try, good luck! Nowadays there are different ways of obtaining payment for not working, and some

MORE ABOUT EMPLOYEES

workers know the ways. With time, you will develop a steady, dependable crew that you can rely on.

Only after employees have proved they are dependable do I allow them to take certain liberties with their time. New employees must be tested before we allow them to make their own hours. Of course, I expect everyone to work hard when there is a lot of work. When times are slack, they can have longer coffee breaks, but they know if they are needed work is the first priority.

Do not fall into the trap of job descriptions.

No newcomers with preconceived ideas from another company! The idea is to improve on what you have experienced. Do not import whatever someone else's immediate suggestion may be. Let them work some time before you ask them whether they have anything new to contribute to their job. Allow your employees to use their ideas. You will be amazed how they can contribute to your company. Of course, I am talking about employees who have been with you for some time.

Do not fall into the trap of job descriptions. Instead, tell your employees they all will learn every phase of

MORE ABOUT EMPLOYEES

the business. They will rotate on their jobs. This will make it more enjoyable for them and will avoid carpal tunnel syndrome problems, etc. since they will not be doing the same motions repetitively. Plus, when one of your employees does not show up to work for whatever reason, you will have replacements who know what to do.

Whenever I walked into the business in the mornings, I had several of my employees come to me with their problems. They usually asked me about problems every few hours, until I told everyone that I could only take care of three problems a day. More would make me lose my temper. Therefore, I would hear about these problems once a day at a certain time. The problems could wait until I gave them my full attention, listen to all of them, and could then take action and solve them.

Also, if I was very busy, my calls would be placed on message notes in their plastic cover, and I would take the time to call back (personally) all of the people who called me. This saved time and I was not interrupted every few minutes. I took care of my calls all at once and could concentrate on everything else. Returning your phone calls yourself—dialing the numbers personally—is an excellent idea and the person you call appreciates it.

INVENTORY

It is almost impossible to keep all the inventory data for small items. And the more effective computerized systems are too expensive and need personnel to control. You are not there yet. At this point you are trying to make do with the least amount of equipment and expenses.

There is no way to know the complete inventory in your business. However, you must pretend to know what you have. This is true about inventory. Make employees aware that you know exactly what is going on in the business, but in fact you cannot know exactly everything to the penny.

By simplifying your storage space with shelves, you will know at a glance what you have. You will know where you are at all times. We keep our stock of cards in boxes on these shelves. We place a card on the outside of each box—easier to spot than numbers—when they are full. When the boxes are empty we turn them around. Simple but effective.

We keep a very organized shop, not just for being neat, but to save time for finding things at a glance. It also avoids producing items you still have on hand.

MANAGING INVENTORY

I cannot stress enough the fact that the larger your inventory, the less money you have in your bank account. Your profits are on the shelves when you need that extra cash.

The more products you have, the larger your stock on hand. This ultimately creates capital formation on your shelves. All your capital is then tied up in inventory.

Clean up your product line, keep only the best sellers.

Regardless of how many choices of products you have, your clients will order only what they have allotted in their mind to buy from your company. Do not forget they need variety and cannot put all their money in your line alone. So clean up your product line, keep only the best sellers, and discard the slow movers. I have been known to destroy poor-selling references worth thousands of dollars.

MANAGING INVENTORY

a story...

Some time ago I had lunch with a very nice artist. We were introduced by our mutual printer. She commented that one of her cards did not move at all, it sat on the clients' shelves. "What would you do?" she asked me. I replied, "Burn them." "What?!" she said, amazed to hear my advice.

"Well, it is the best suggestion I can give you. First, if it is a dog (i.e., a poor seller) you do not want your customers to be stuck with an image that is known to be a poor seller. It will reflect badly on your line.

"Second, for your own peace of mind, you do not want to walk into your place of business daily and be faced with an item that does not sell well and is taking up valuable space. Go on to the next project and forget the bad sellers. BURN THEM!"

Nowadays, whenever we meet she greets me with "Burn them!"

MANAGING INVENTORY

a story...

At my first trade show with my cards, I received an order from Canada. They had chosen many styles, among them one that was a poor seller. My assistant, who knew how many I had on hand, said, "Good, we are going to get rid of many of these cards." I mentioned to her that upon reviewing their order, I was not going to ship them that reference since it was a poor seller. She could not believe me. Presumably she thought I was not a good salesperson.

After 17 years, we are still distributed in Canada by this same company. So who was right?

MANUFACTURE LESS

Your suppliers will tell you that it is less expensive to order larger amounts and gain discounts. That is true, but ask them to break down the prices in three ways, for 1000, 2000, 3000 units, or whichever amount you want to check.

You will find out that larger quantities' costs are lower. Then consider that larger amounts require 1) more storage area, 2) more capital invested. If your product is seasonal, imagine keeping it on hand for the next season.

Never base your margin of profit on larger quantities where you obtain more discounts. If your business grows very fast, you may need larger quantities where you can save on these discounts. But do not forget that your break-even costs will also increase accordingly as you enlarge your space of business, number of employees, etc.

Just manufacture a reasonable amount. Better less than more. It is so much better to fill inventories with best sellers than to look at stock that just sits there. You will gain additional space and have more liquid capital. Therefore, just manufacture less. Repeat the best sellers and liquidate or destroy the slow movers.

INVENTORY CONTROL

I will repeat it again: The larger your inventory, the less money you have in your bank account. You can establish inventory controls using the computer where it is done automatically when printing invoices. But we are focusing here on a small business that starts with limited resources and cannot afford either the time or personnel required to have all these controls, or for whom the computer systems cost too much to purchase and maintain. At this point you want something that will do the job fast and easy.

The larger your inventory, the less money you have in your bank account.

It is a rare employee who will advise you within plenty of time when you are getting low on some items. You should check your inventories in a routine fashion. I periodically walk through the aisles of my merchandise shelves and make a visual check, marking items that need to be restocked.

SHIPPING SUGGESTIONS

Here are some suggestions on how to handle shipping as a small company. These ideas can help you get organized and avoid mistakes, save time, and limit claims on orders not being filled properly.

For my card company, we ordered tables 4' x 8'. In the center we placed two shelf units attached to the tables (the shelves were 8' x 24"). The shelves are elevated, allowing the use of the full table. One operator works on one side and another on the other side. Supplies are arranged on the overhead shelves as well as in the shelving under the tables, which is also used as storage.

Employees work from orders and place the various items in front. By laying out the different references (products) ordered, we can spot mistakes and avoid duplicating quantities and references. It is very easy to spot this. The order is then placed in a container with its respective printed invoice. Before releasing this order to the shipping desk, the order is again checked, matching the printed invoice to the original (sales representative's order).

The shipping clerk checks the order for the third time. During all this process our employees sign a little card

SHIPPING SUGGESTIONS

(in the most shocking color) which we enclose with the order. The card says:

      Counted by _____
      Checked by _____
      Packed by _____

Avoid clutter. Try to keep your paper work at a minimum. Many of the lessons I learned repeatedly taught me not to complicate anything in business. SIMPLIFY, SIMPLIFY, SIMPLIFY.

SHIPPING SUGGESTIONS

a story...

One of our sales representatives once ordered cards for his daughter's wedding. We shipped to his home. He called us all excited. It was the first time he saw how we packed our cards and he was so impressed. Of course, we have to keep our image and show our clients how much we care about our product.

We divide the various sizes with cardboard. We wrap smaller cards in tissue paper. We cover this with tissue and place a foam core piece on the top. Our cartons are made to order with our logo, and we pay additional money for extra heavy cardboard and complete flaps.

A SIMPLE IDEA

How much is your time and your employees' time worth? This idea involves a small expenditure of less than $100, but it will save your company hundreds of dollars. There is nothing more frustrating than having scraps of paper all over. This idea eliminates that problem and helps you avoid duplicating orders.

Simply purchase clear plastic sleeves which open on two sides. Every note, memo, bill, invoice, whatever needs to be done in your office, is placed inside these sleeves, no matter how small the piece of paper is.

The original invoice is protected by this plastic sleeve. Once you receive an order via mail, phone, fax, etc., you place the order in one of these sleeves. When you finish typing the order, place the original together with the final order in the sleeve. In this way you can be sure that you will not lose orders and all the papers are together.

Such a simple idea and so cheap—yet you will appreciate this helpful, time-saving organizer.

FILING SYSTEMS

Whenever I hire people, they look around wondering where the file cabinets are. Our bookkeeper has only two, one with four drawers and one with two. How can we do this, you may ask?

Many years ago I attended a trade show in Dallas with several other manufacturers. As is usual, we all exchanged ideas and information.

One young couple showing their jewelry line were very nice. I engaged the young man in conversation and was amazed that so young a man had such a successful business. I asked him how many people he employed in his shop and office. When he responded that he only had one secretary and his lovely young wife in their office, I asked him how they did it. He volunteered to have his wife explain to me how they managed with just two people doing all the paper work. They moved a lot of merchandise.

She was very generous with her information, and I asked her whether I could take notes. She told me it was so simple. It is simple, yes, but I did not know about this way of managing an office before. When I returned home, I did away with my old system and started her way. Even as my business grew in volume,

FILING SYSTEMS

this procedure has served me well and still does. Here is what she taught me.

The whole system resides in having your invoices printed in four copies of different colors:

ORIGINAL: Usually white, which is mailed to your client.

SECOND: Usually yellow and used as a packing slip that is attached to the carton in the packing slip envelopes with transparent tops to avoid mistakes.

THIRD: Usually orange and filed in the sales representative's folder with their order, fax, paper work attached to it.

FOURTH: Usually pink. This is our "Bible." These are kept in consecutive numerical order.

This fourth copy is our working copy. Whatever happens with this order—questions, shortages, returns, etc.—is written on this copy. This is the copy we stamp PAID with a stamp that also prints the date. We file these copies by month, attaching a card on the spine of the file where we write the month, beginning and last number of the invoices.

Before the computer age we transferred the name,

FILING SYSTEMS

address, invoice number, date, etc., on a Rolodex file which we kept updating every day. By keeping only cards in alphabetical order, we avoided individual files for customers. We opened individual files only for very large accounts.

This system keeps our records always at hand and up-to-date. There is no need to spend time searching—everything is in its place.

FILING SYSTEMS

a story...

This excellent idea was suggested by my niece. She once asked me, "What do you do with the orders your salespeople mail to you?" I replied that we filed them. "I suggest," she said, "to do as we do. Just attach all their papers and correspondence with their commission check, and send these papers back to them. Otherwise you will be swamped with paperwork."

We implemented this suggestion right away. Our files were already bulging with paper. By using this system we keep in the respective sales people's file unpaid orders plus a single sheet for the month noting the invoice number, customer and commission paid. This way we can refer to the single sheet of monthly transactions and by having the invoice number listed, all we have to do is go to our Bible, "the pinks," and find the answers.

FILING SYSTEMS

a story...

Limit paperwork. I cannot emphasize this enough. I just fired a secretary who decided to reorganize my company her way. Our sales were one-third of what our previous secretaries took care of, yet this one was always so busy she needed an assistant!

Knowing how much time this work must take, I fired her. When I opened one of her drawers, I had to throw away about 20 files. First, they were not tagged to show their contents. Second, everything was duplicated. For instance, if one of our clients sent us a change of address, she saved the paper. She had entered this information in the computer, so why keep the paper?

COMPUTERS

When starting a business, money is quite tight. Seventeen years ago, computers were not as popular as they are today, and they were much more expensive. Besides, the software required was extremely costly.

I attended several courses and learned the history of computers plus got a lot of information which at that time I was not interested in. All I was interested in was how to put the growing names of our accounts in alphabetical order to avoid entering this information in my Rolodex. This was becoming tedious and time-consuming. By using the computer it became so easy to change the address, zip codes, whatever, and they were always in perfect alphabetical order.

At that time I could already afford a computer, but how to learn? A business friend of mine recommended a young person who would teach me how to operate the computer if I bought it from him. When this young man arrived, I was overwhelmed with the boxes of books he brought in. I then told him right away that all I wanted the machine to do for me was keep my customers' list in alphabetical order, to please just teach me that.

COMPUTERS

He was amazed because the machine could do so many more things, and here I was, requesting one function only. Besides, here I was—the owner—who was going to learn how to use this machine!

As I have often repeated, I feel it is necessary to know how everything works. To train my secretary to use the computer—which was the approach he usually took—was not my style. Secretaries come and go, but you always remain in your business.

I told him that as soon as I learned about my lists, I would then call him again to come teach me other applications.

Computers are a wonderful tool, and they really save personnel and time, but trying to learn how to operate them all at once is not the best way.

Rozy's Rules

1
You must be single minded and completely immersed in your work.

2
Remember if you do not face a problem it will not go away.

3
A tight budget keeps you focused and controlled.

4
Never hire friends or relatives.

NOTES:

ORDER FORM

❑ Please send me
"Let Me Help You with Your Business"
_____ copies @ $19.95 each.   _____

                                   Shipping* _____
                        TOTAL ENCLOSED _____

❑ Please send me information on:
   ❑ Speaking/Seminars Available
   ❑ Consulting Services

*SHIPPING:
   US: $4.00 for first book, $2.00 for each additional book.
   International: $9.00 for first book, $5.00 for each additional copy.

Name: _____

Address: _____

_____

City: _____ State: _____ Zip: _____

Telephone: _____

E-mail: _____

Send check or money order payable to

Rozy Inc.
815 Sand Ave
Eugene, Or. 97401
T:541 344-1939/Fax:541 342-5278